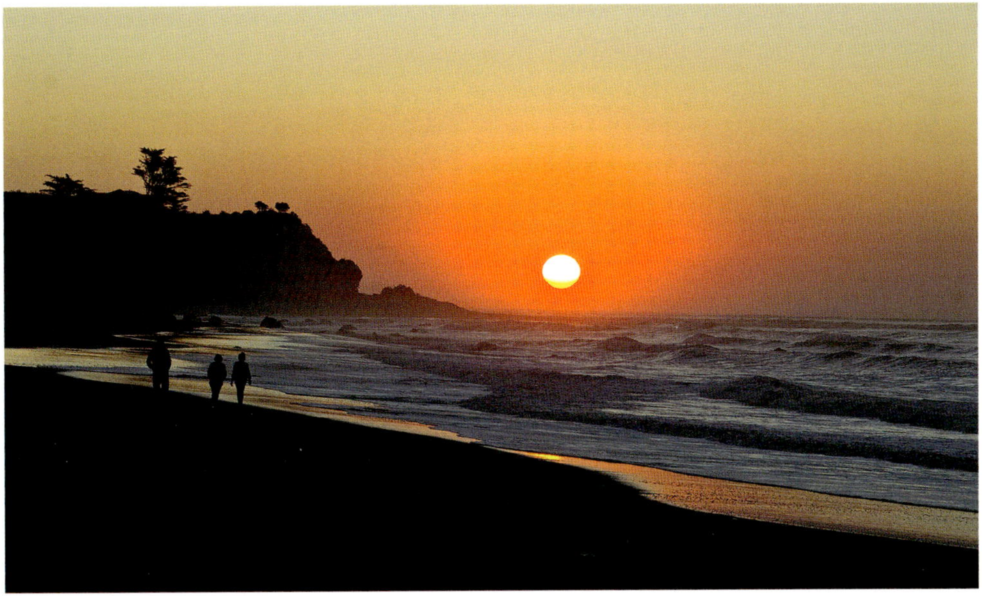

The Real New Zealand

Fay Looney

NEW HOLLAND

On a good day, dawn can arrive in an explosion of colour. It's not something I can ever plan for, but I'm always thankful for being there when it happens. With luck, patience – and by getting out of bed early – you might just experience an unforgettable moment.

Dawn light can ignite the pohutukawa that bloom in season along our coastline and the nikau palms that march beside the beaches down south. Through the progress of a day, the changes in colour can be dramatic, and often just plain gorgeous. As the day unfolds moody shadows of grey arrive on mountain tops and beaches in the form of fluffy clouds that are pierced by great shafts of light, all of which brings inspiration to photographers like me.

Cape Reinga gave me the moment, and conditions were perfect as we watched the sky turn pastel colours. It was bad luck that it poured with rain at Waitangi, but it didn't stop me wading into the sea to capture those magnificent waka crews putting their heart and soul into pushing their large craft through the murky conditions.

This landscape has shaped the people of New Zealand; their many interests and skills are drawn from an agricultural heritage that can be seen reflected in the unique celebrations, shows, art festivals and activities that I seek throughout the country.

My mission is to tempt you there … then to go back for more.

This little book is dedicated to all of you who have encouraged me to see:
Harry for the miles we have shared; and our grandchildren, Sam, Lauren, Harry jnr., Mack, Ben and Kate (my able assistant).

Fay Looney

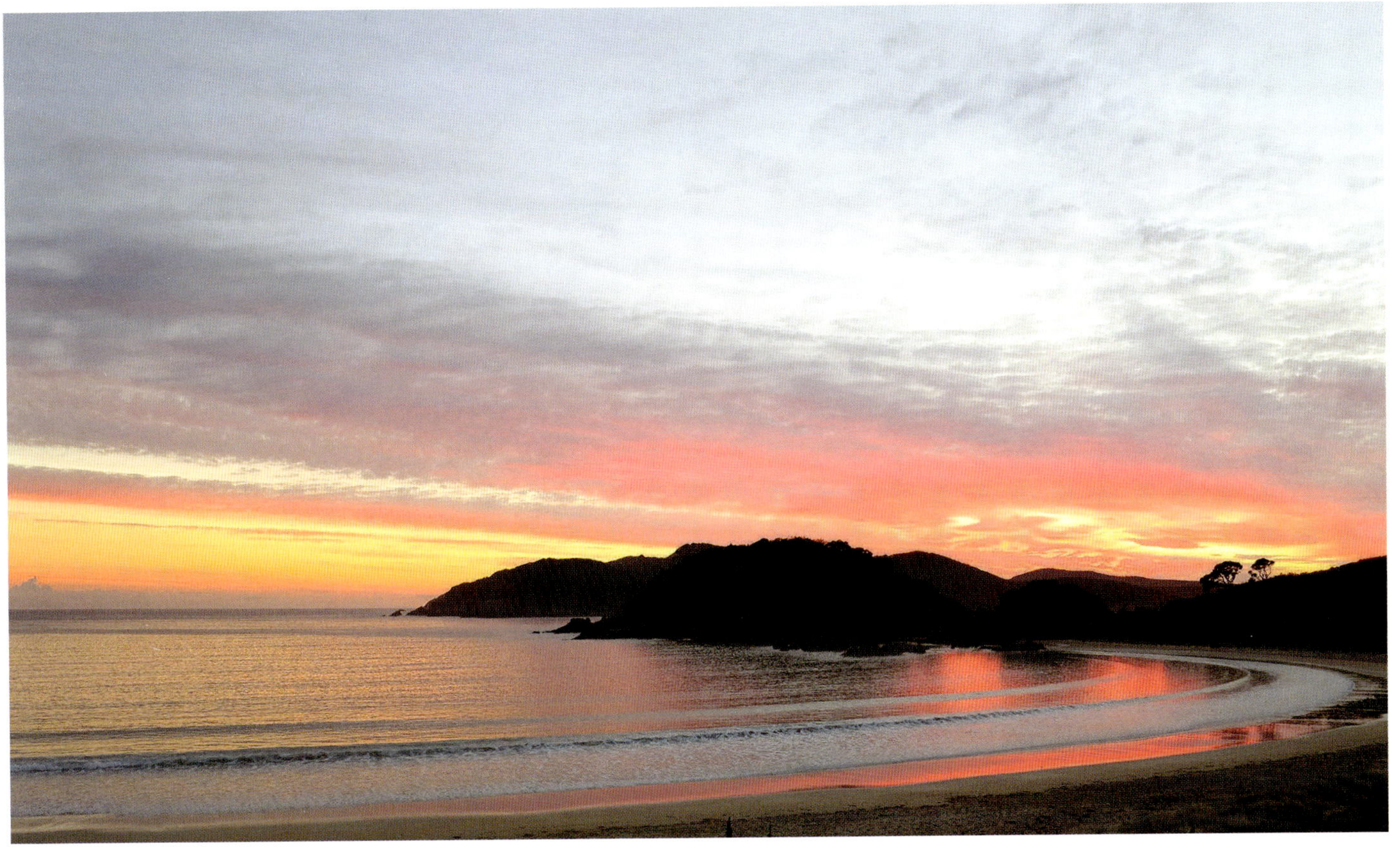

▲ Matai Bay, Karikari Peninsula. Nature's paintbrush touches lightly on this remote Northland bay.

◀◀ Oakura Beach, where the sun lingers (and where I live).

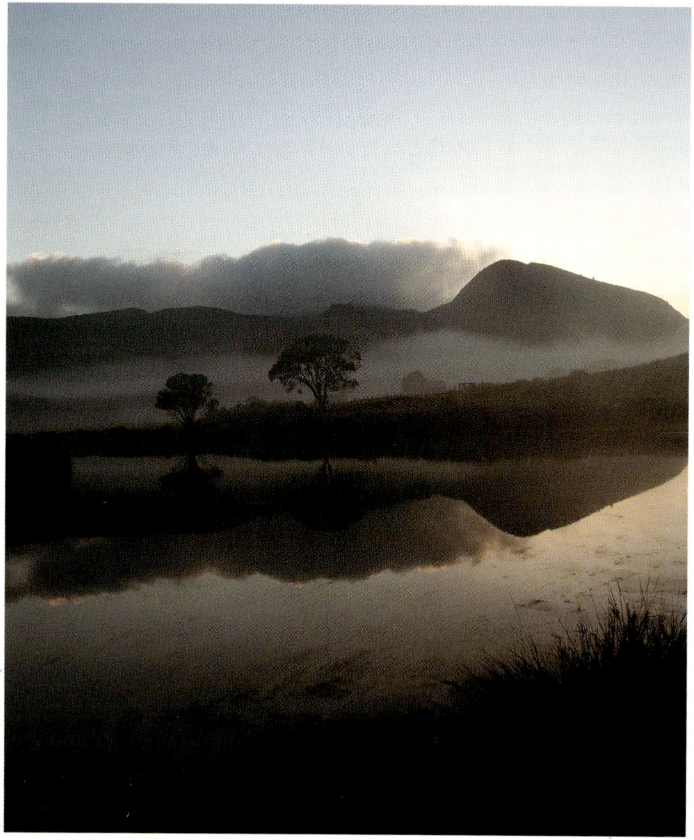

▲ Spirits (Piwhane) Bay, Far North – a place sacred to Maori, seen here through the drifting sea fog.

▶ Cape Reinga. Here the often-stormy Tasman Sea merges seamlessly with the mighty Pacific Ocean.

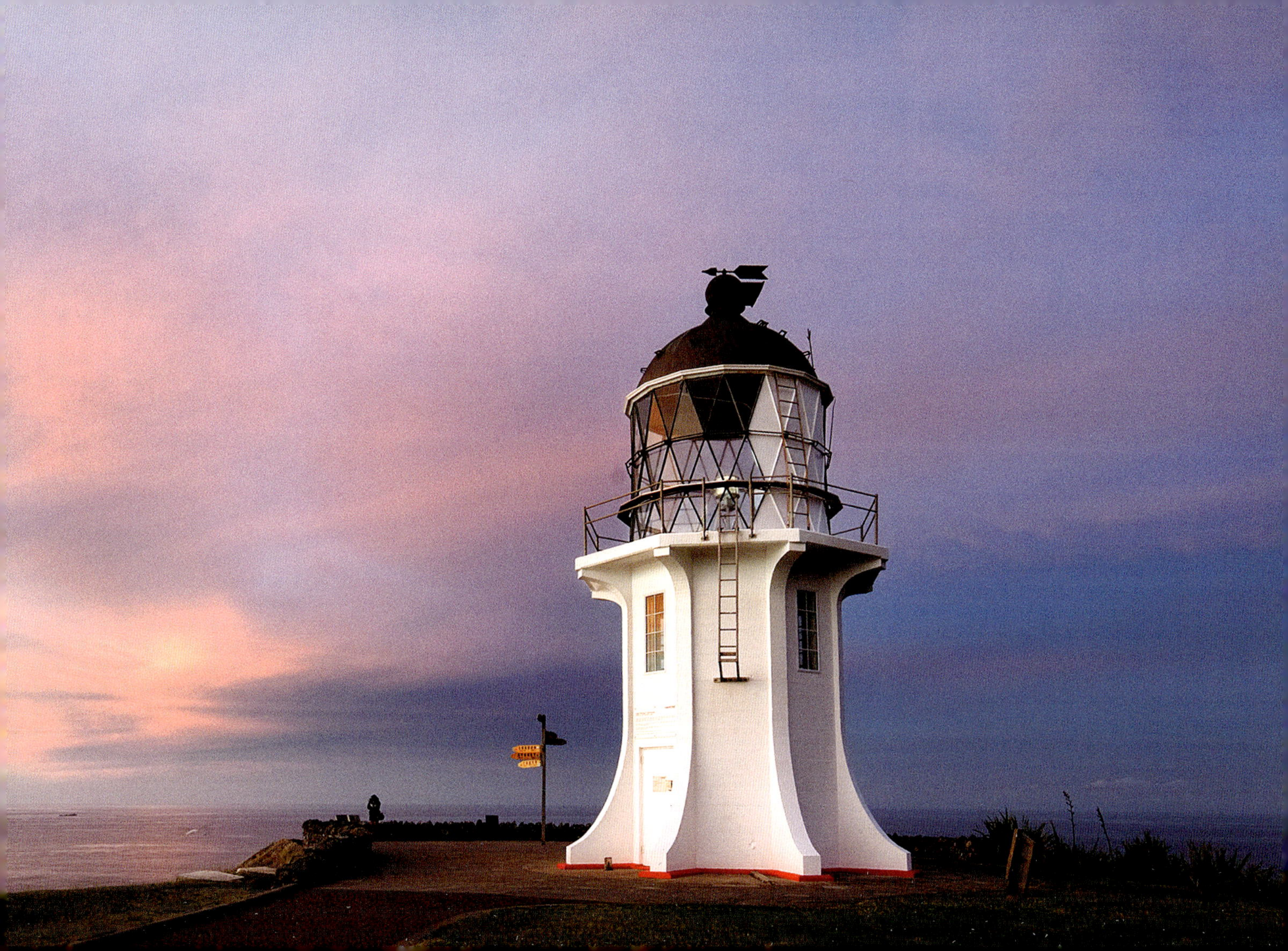

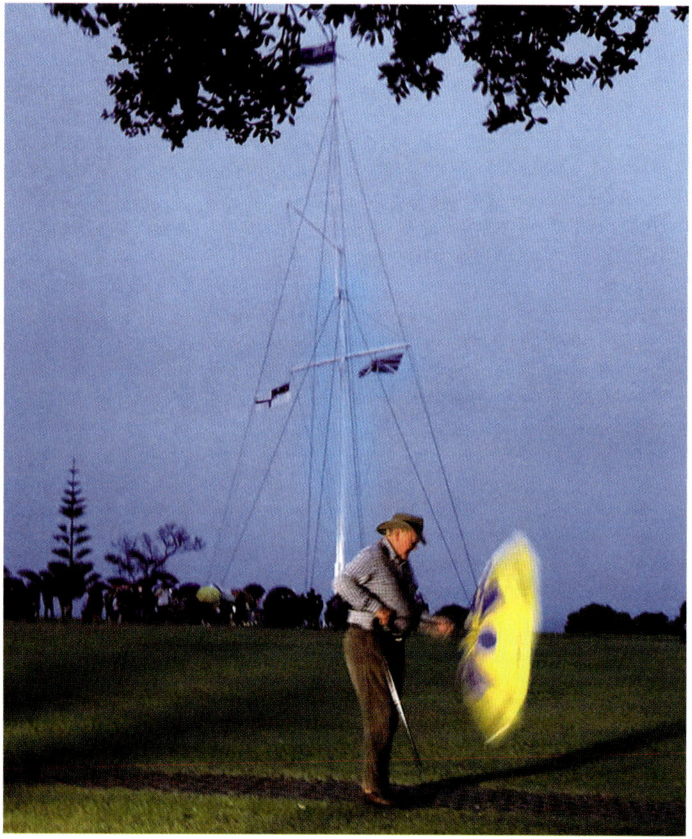

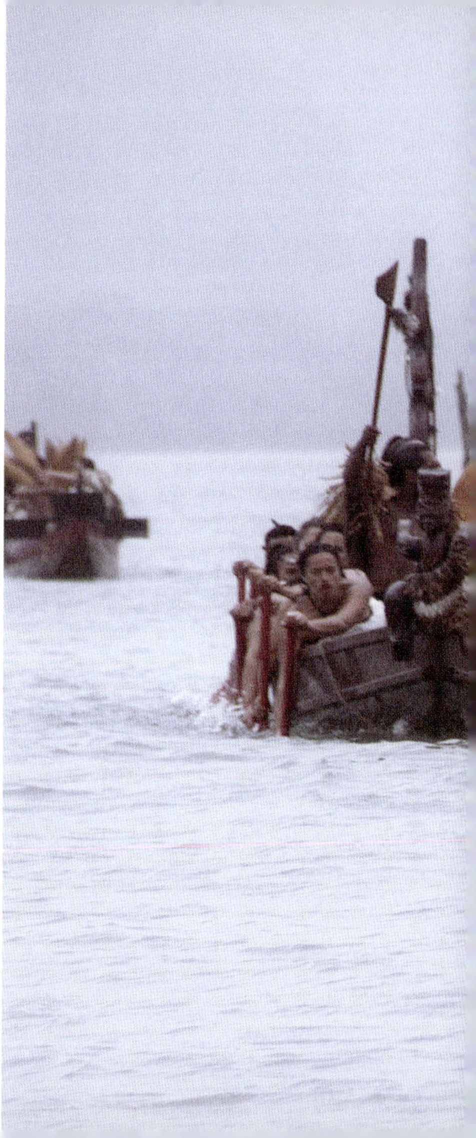

▲ Waitangi Treaty Grounds, Bay of Islands. Wet and windy weather is no deterrent for those making the annual pilgrimage to honour New Zealand's great founding document, the Treaty of Waitangi.

▶ Ceremonial waka crews deliver a heart-racing spectacle.

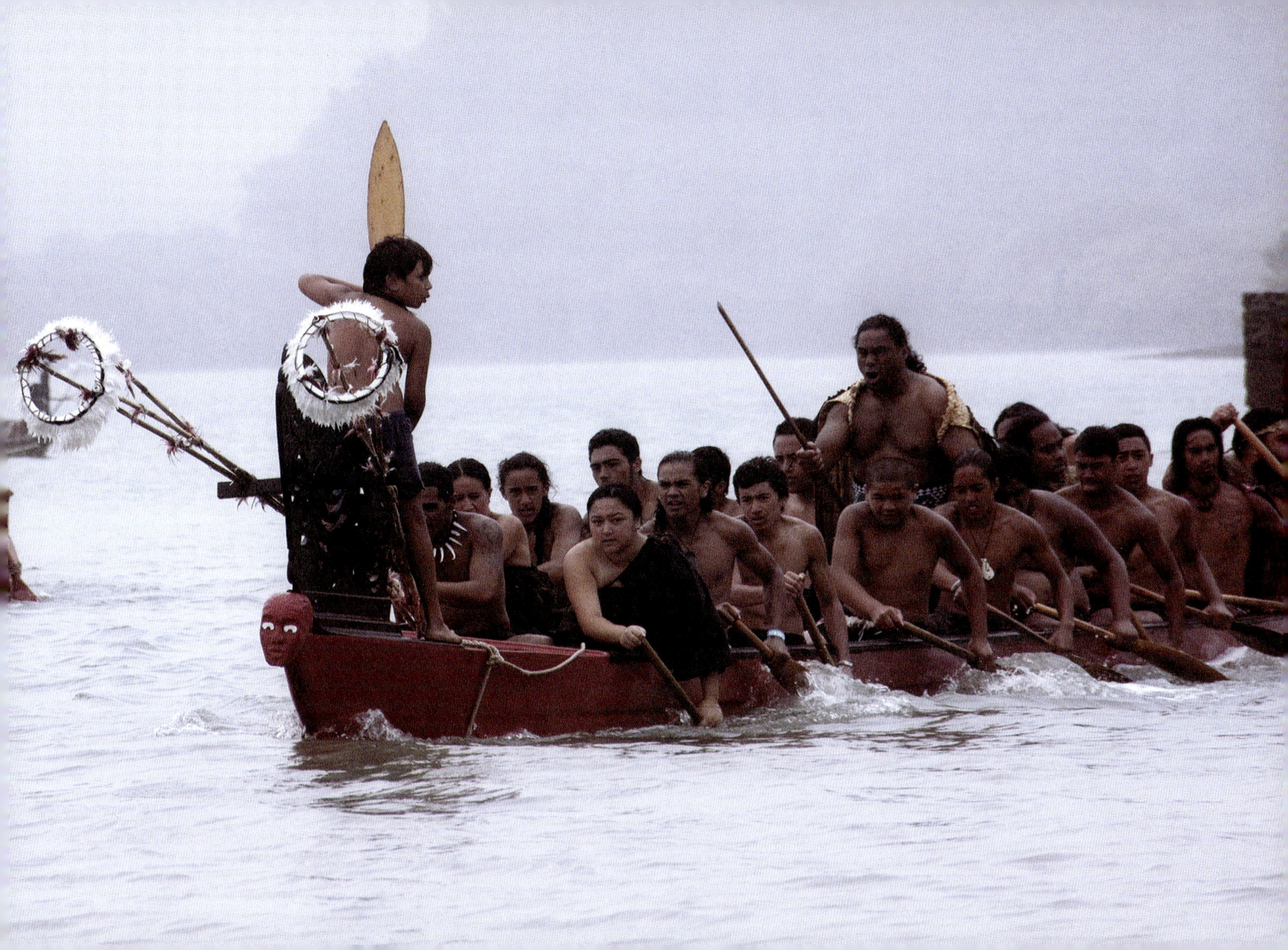

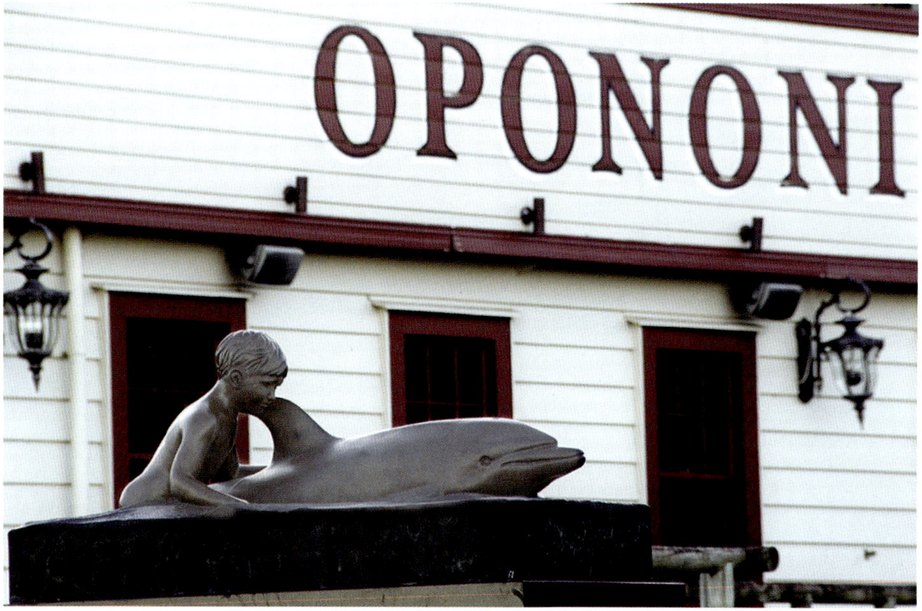

▲ Opo the friendly dolphin was for some years an icon of the North. Although long departed, the memory of his smile and playful antics lives on.

▶ This pohutukawa in full flower at Opononi near the mouth of the Hokianga in the Far North is a reminder to all passing Kiwis when it blooms that Christmas can't be far away.

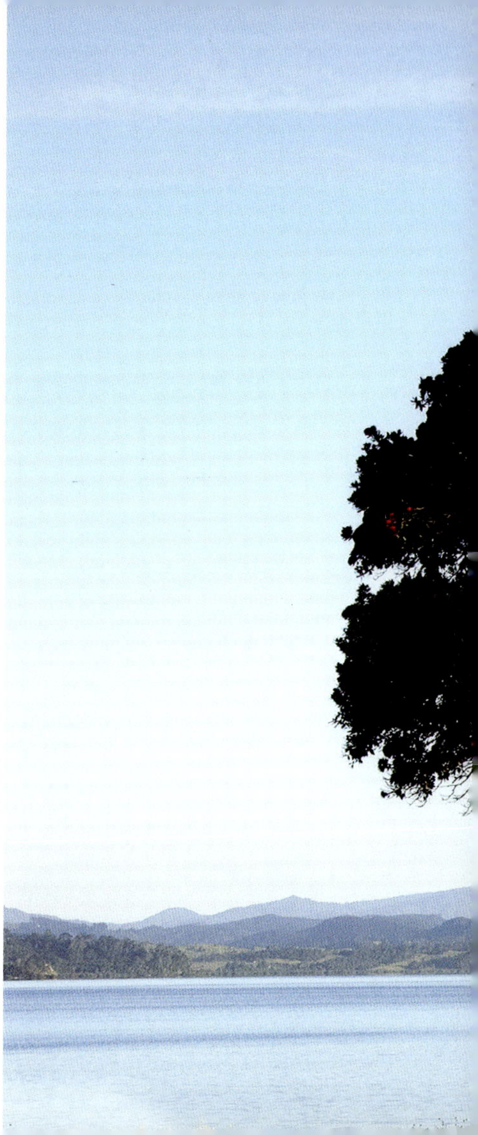

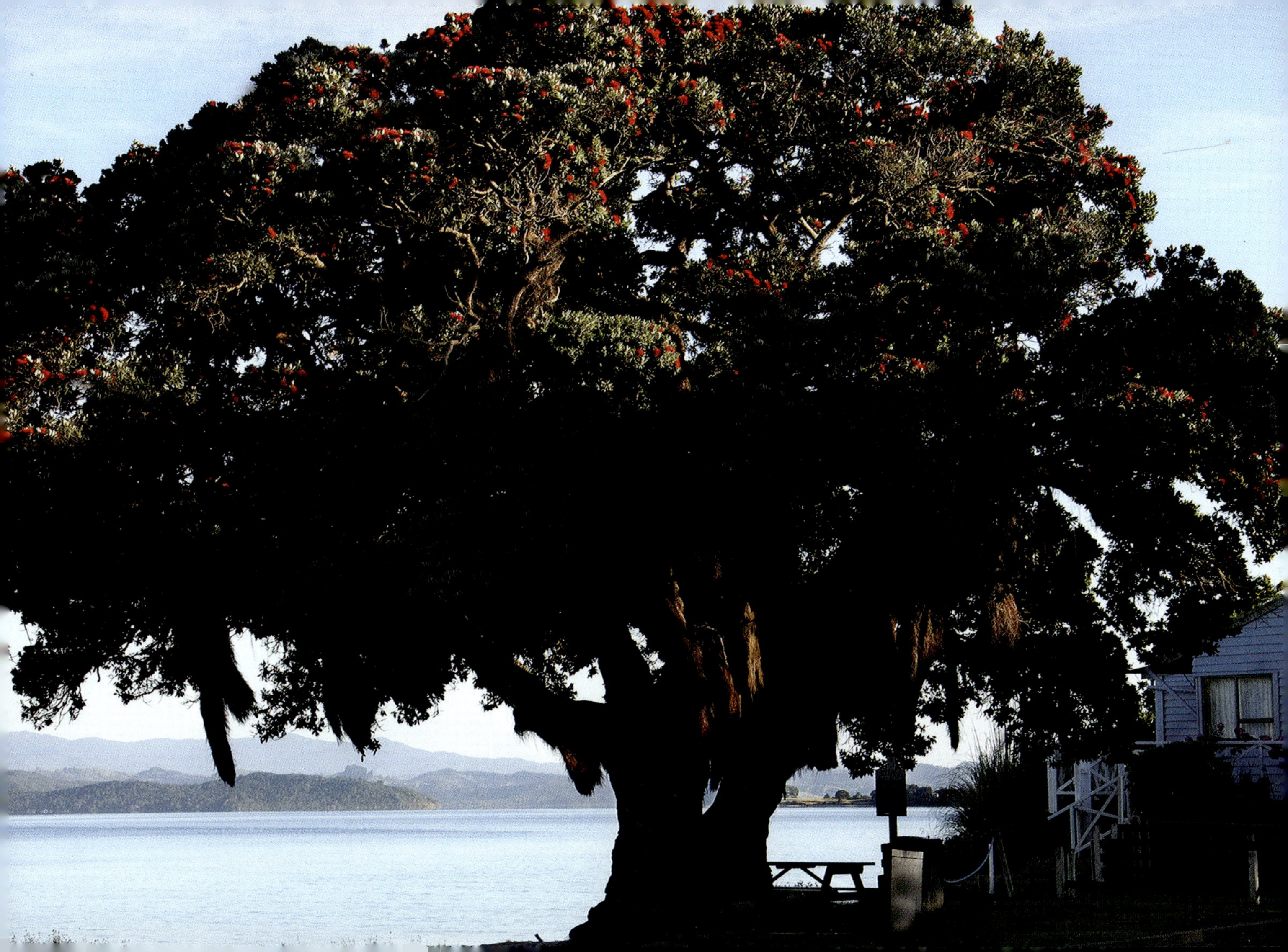

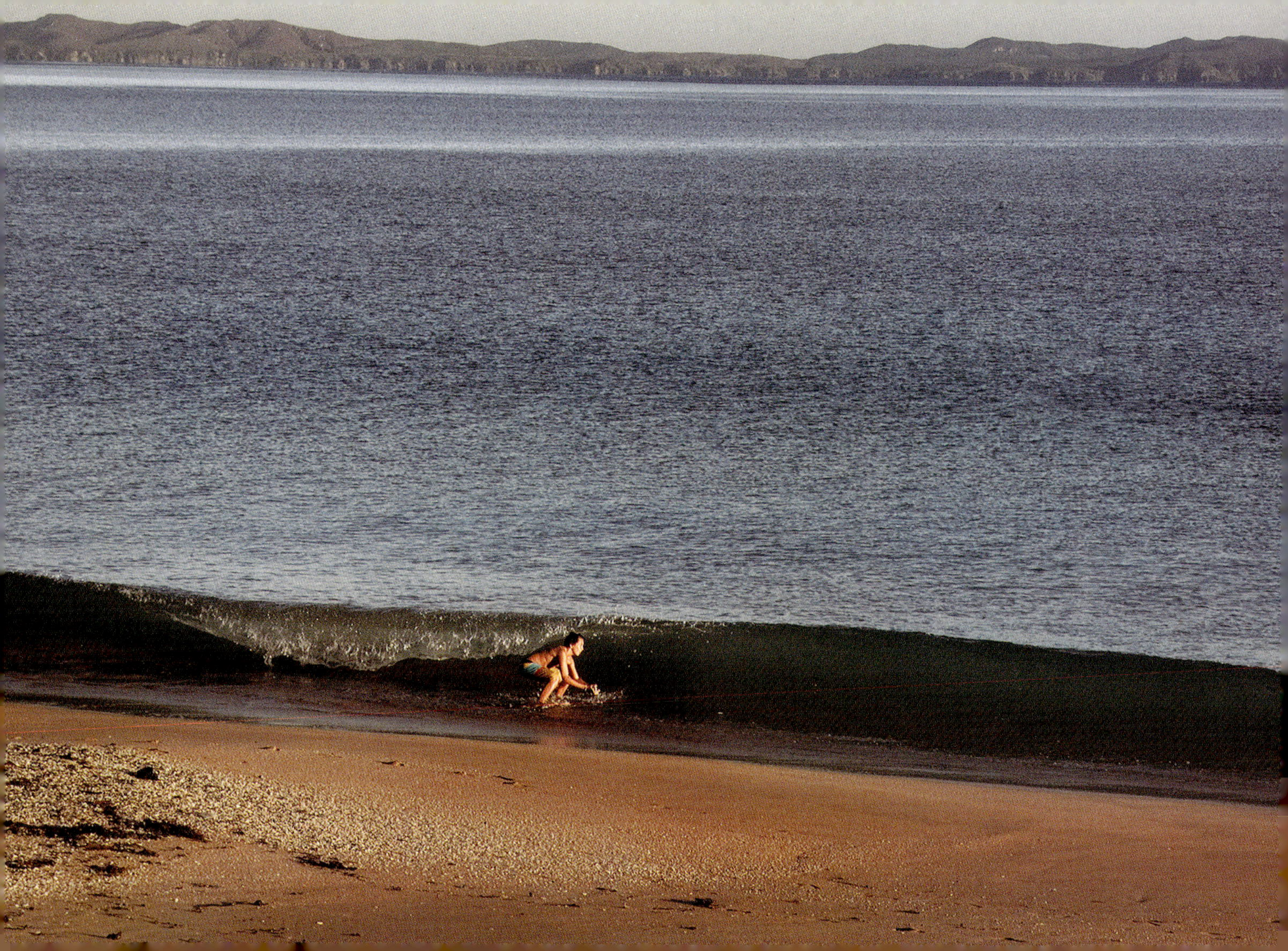

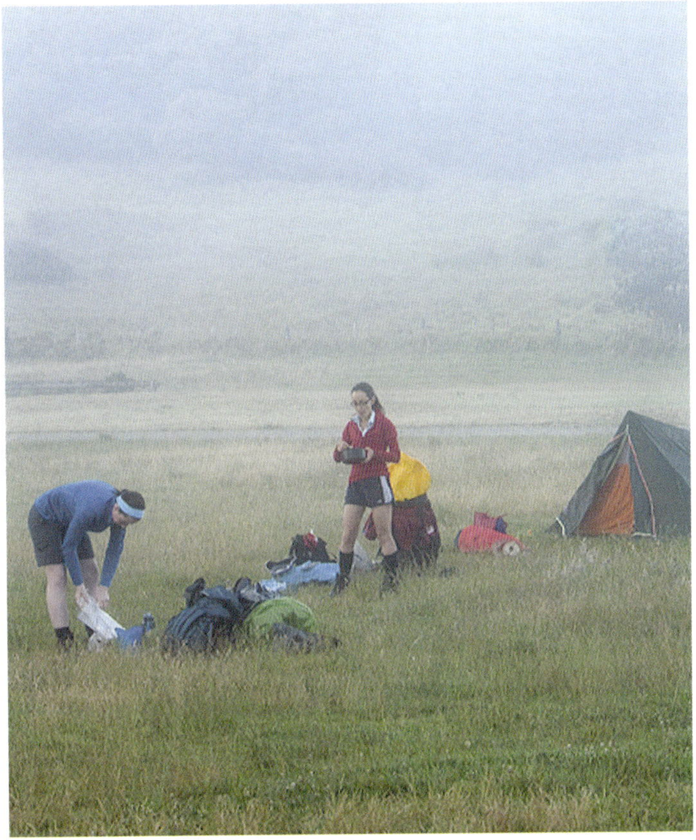

▲ Spirits (Piwhane) Bay where the lifting mists are a reminder of the spirits believed to gather here before departing to the afterlife.

◀ Coopers Beach, Far North. An early morning beach break folds this youngster into its barrel, as he dreams of the big one.

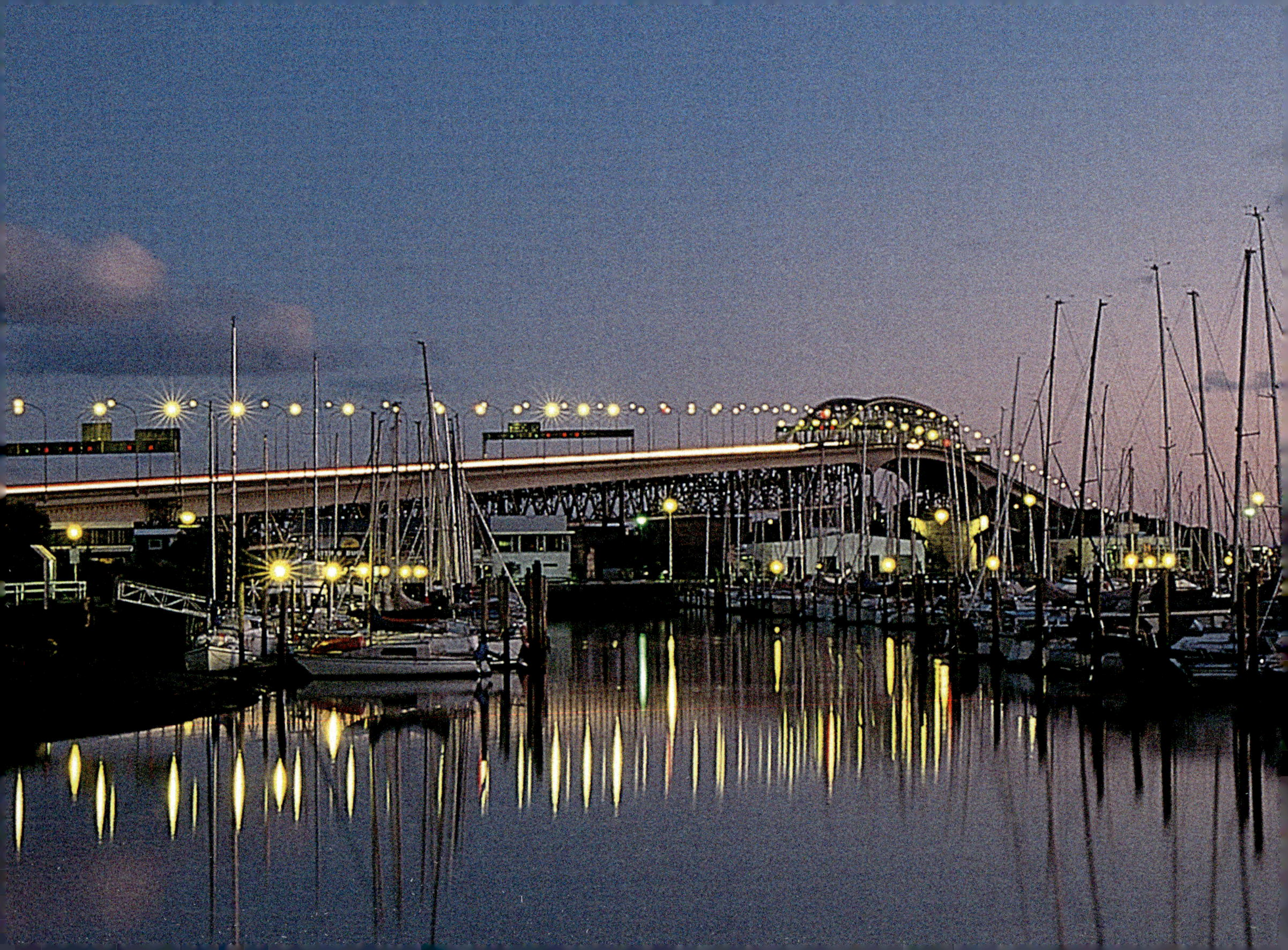

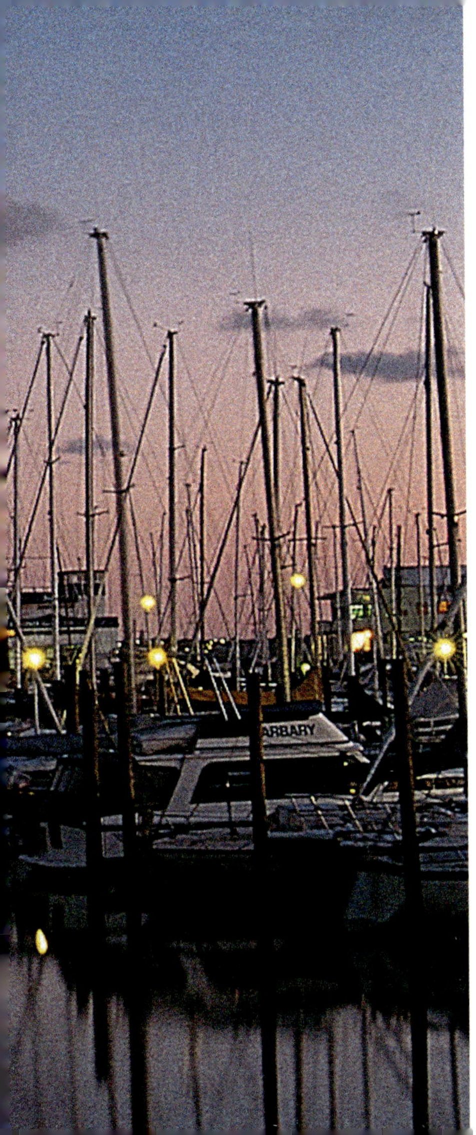

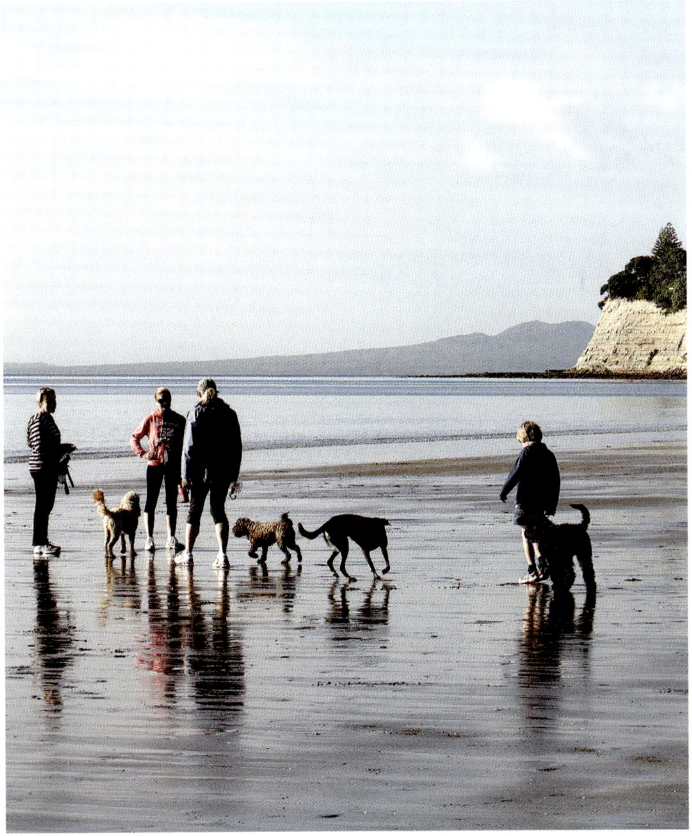

▲ Early morning at Long Bay on Auckland's North Shore, where dogs and neighbours catch up before the working day begins.

◀ Westhaven Marina. Auckland's northern gateway is illuminated and softened in the warm light of dawn.

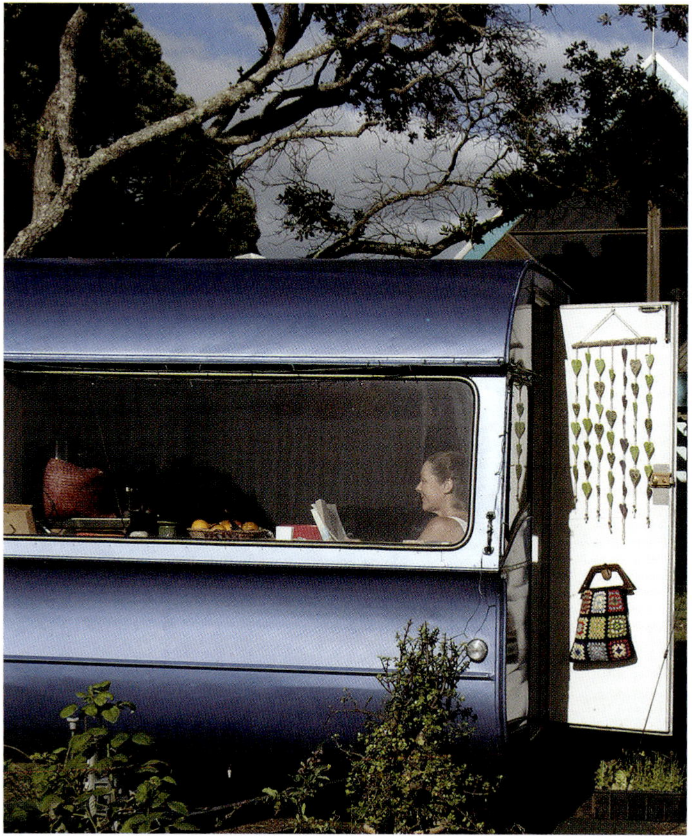

▲ Orewa Holiday Park, north of Auckland, where perfect peace can be found in a home away from home.

▶ Gulf Harbour, Whangaparaoa, offers an overnight park with a million-dollar view.

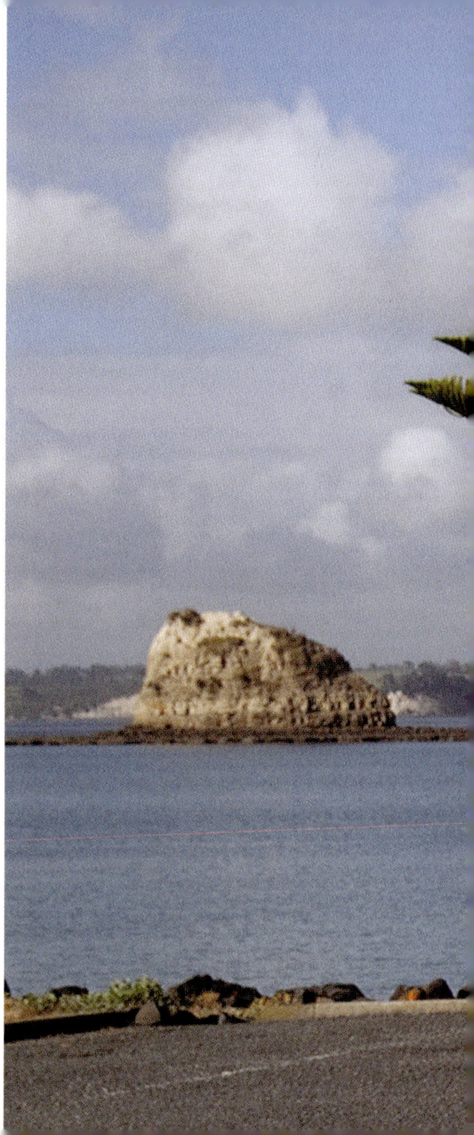

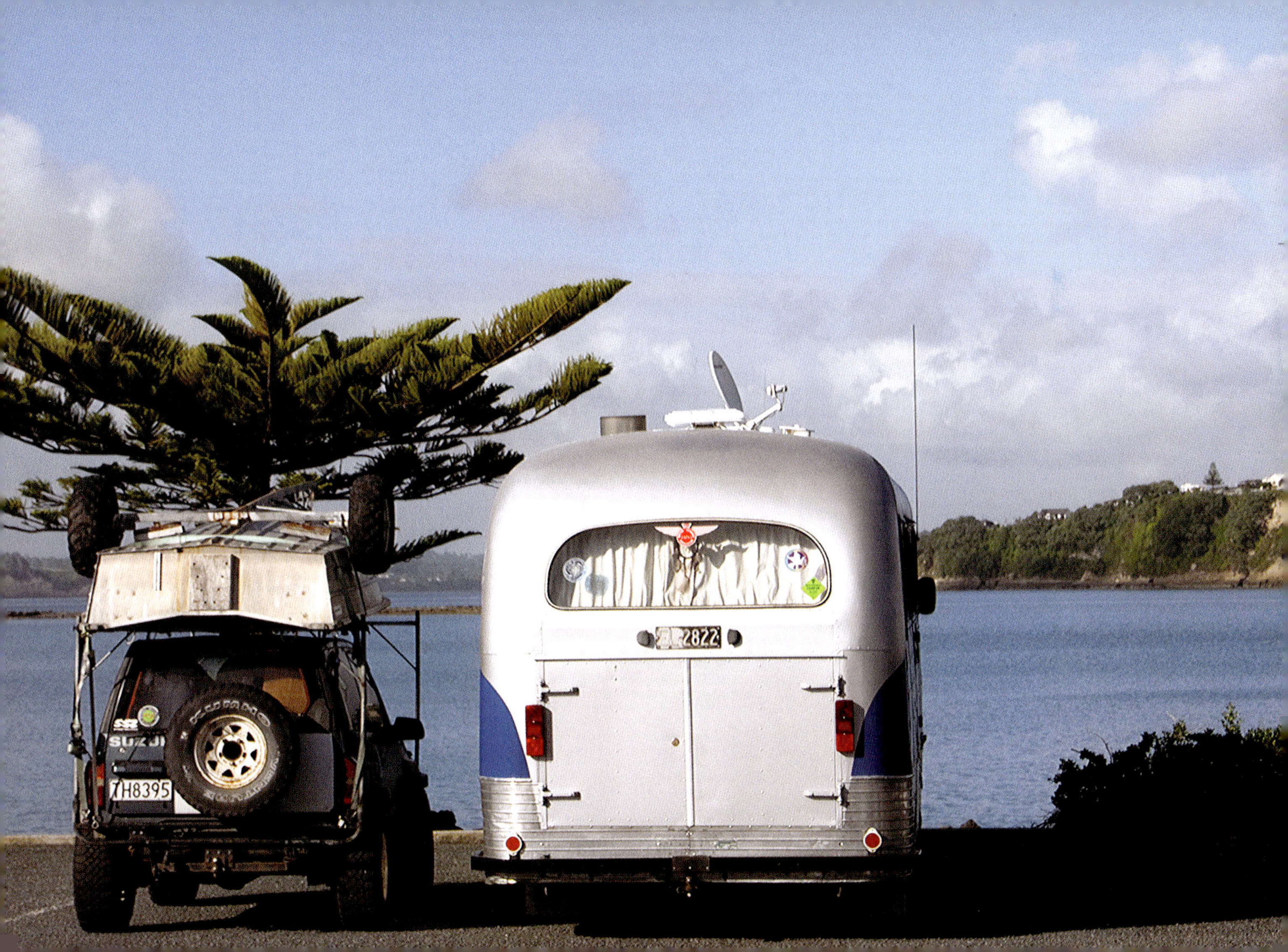
TH8395
2822

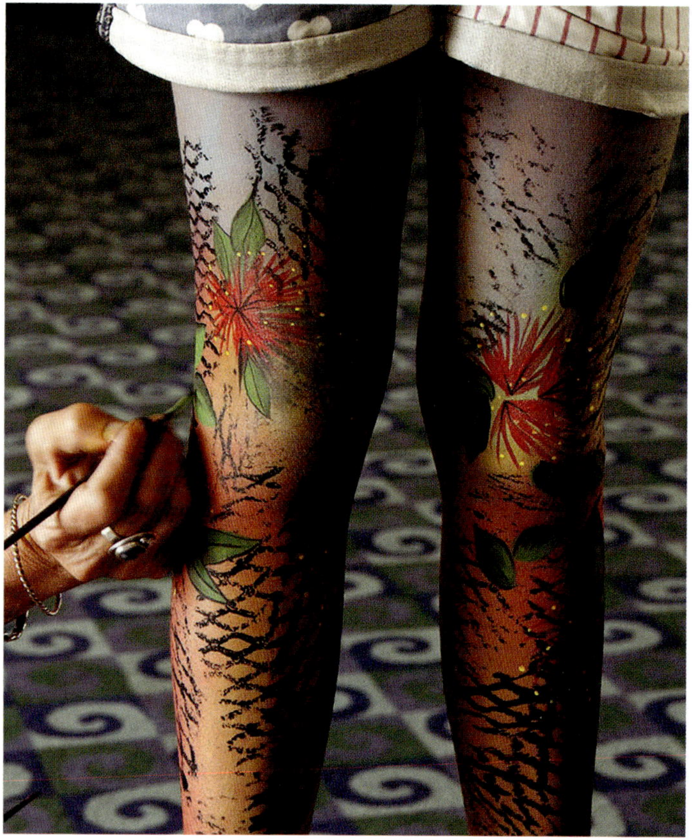

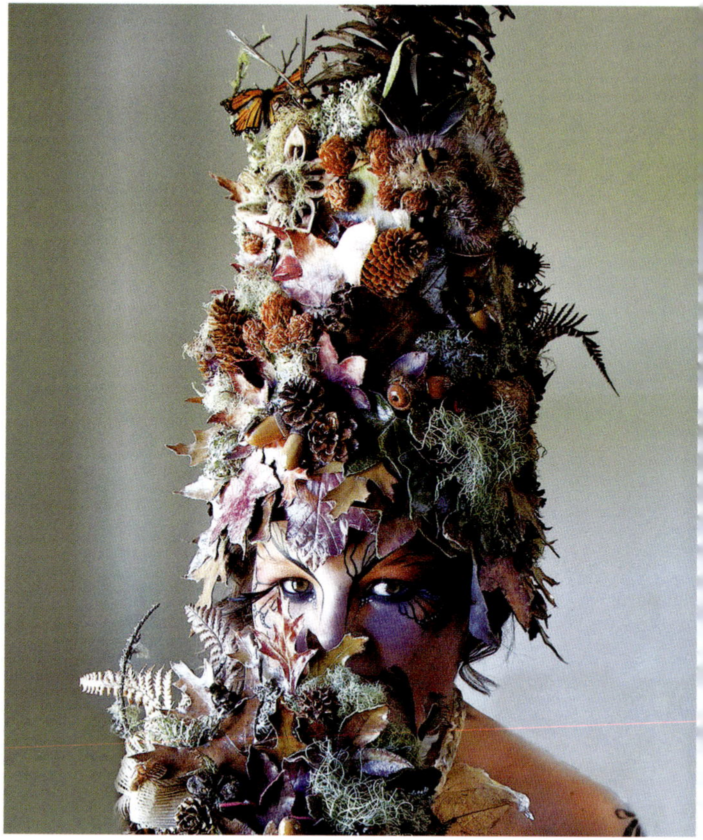

▲ The annual Pohutukawa Festival at Thames, the gateway to the Coromandel Peninsula, allows creative mothers to turn summer fantasies into wearable art.

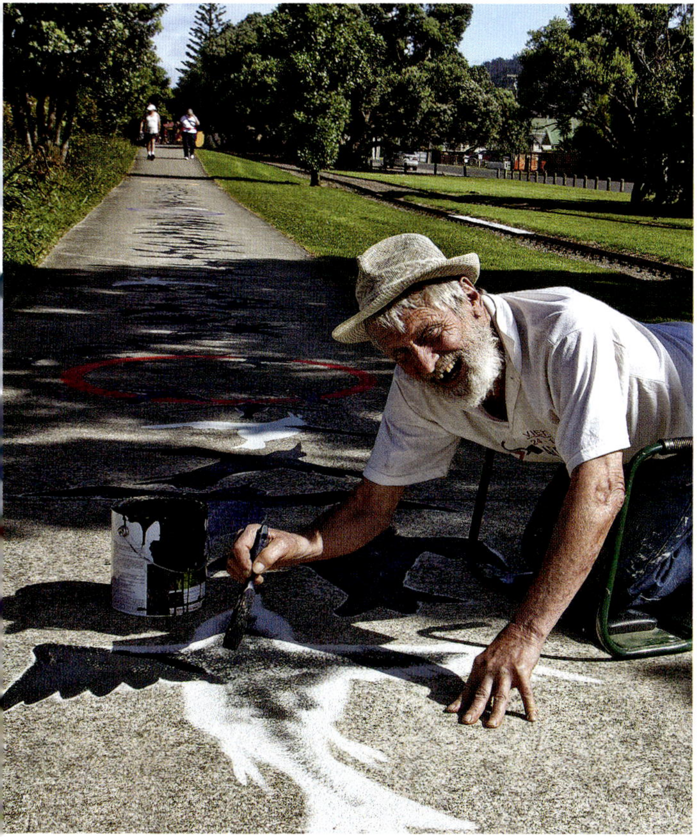

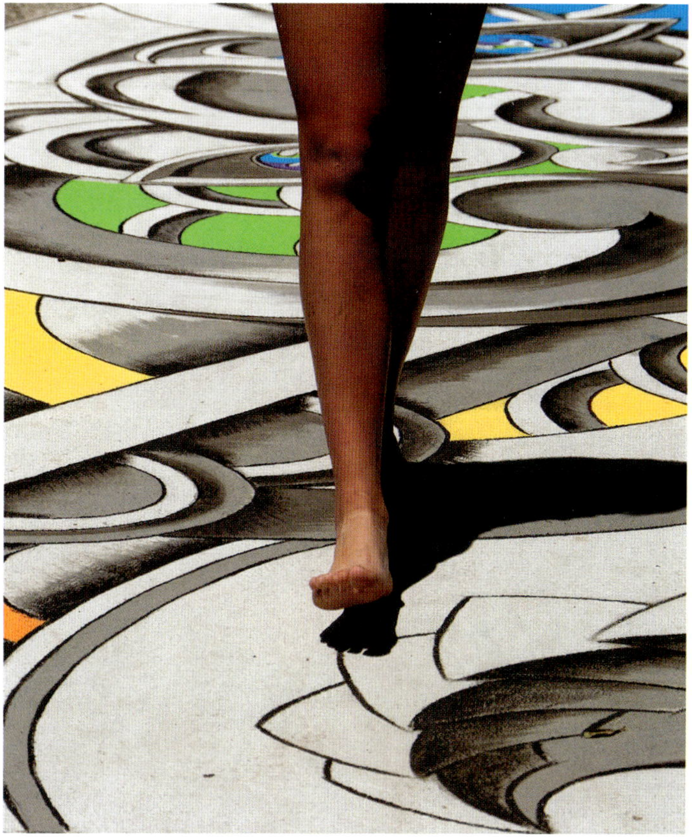

▲ At that same festival local celebrities are encouraged to lend a hand to transform a concrete walkway into a colourful canvas.

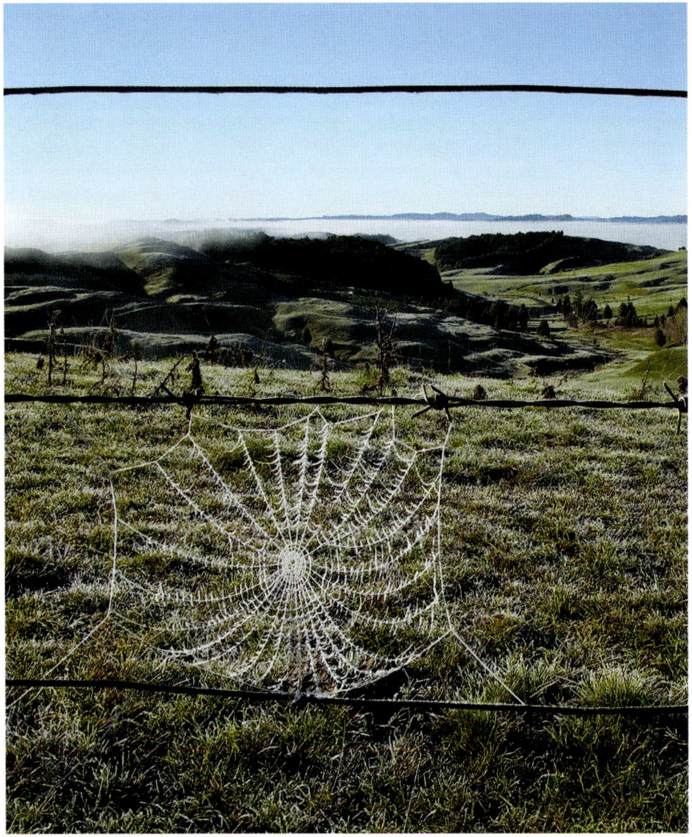

▲ This spiderweb, crystalline with frost, frames a section of Waitomo farmland with the Mahoenui hills in the background.

▶ Otorohanga's shiny kiwi welcomes northbound travellers and offers shelter to its mates.

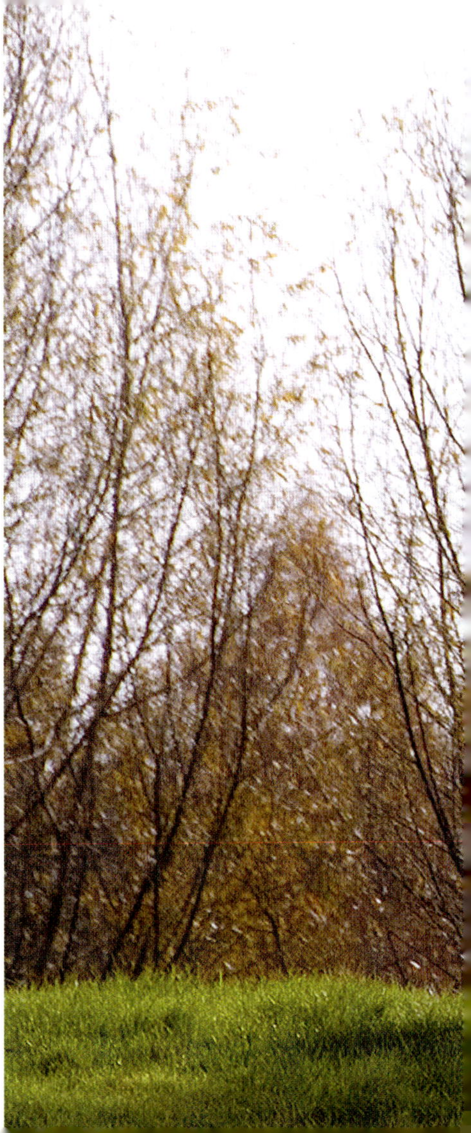

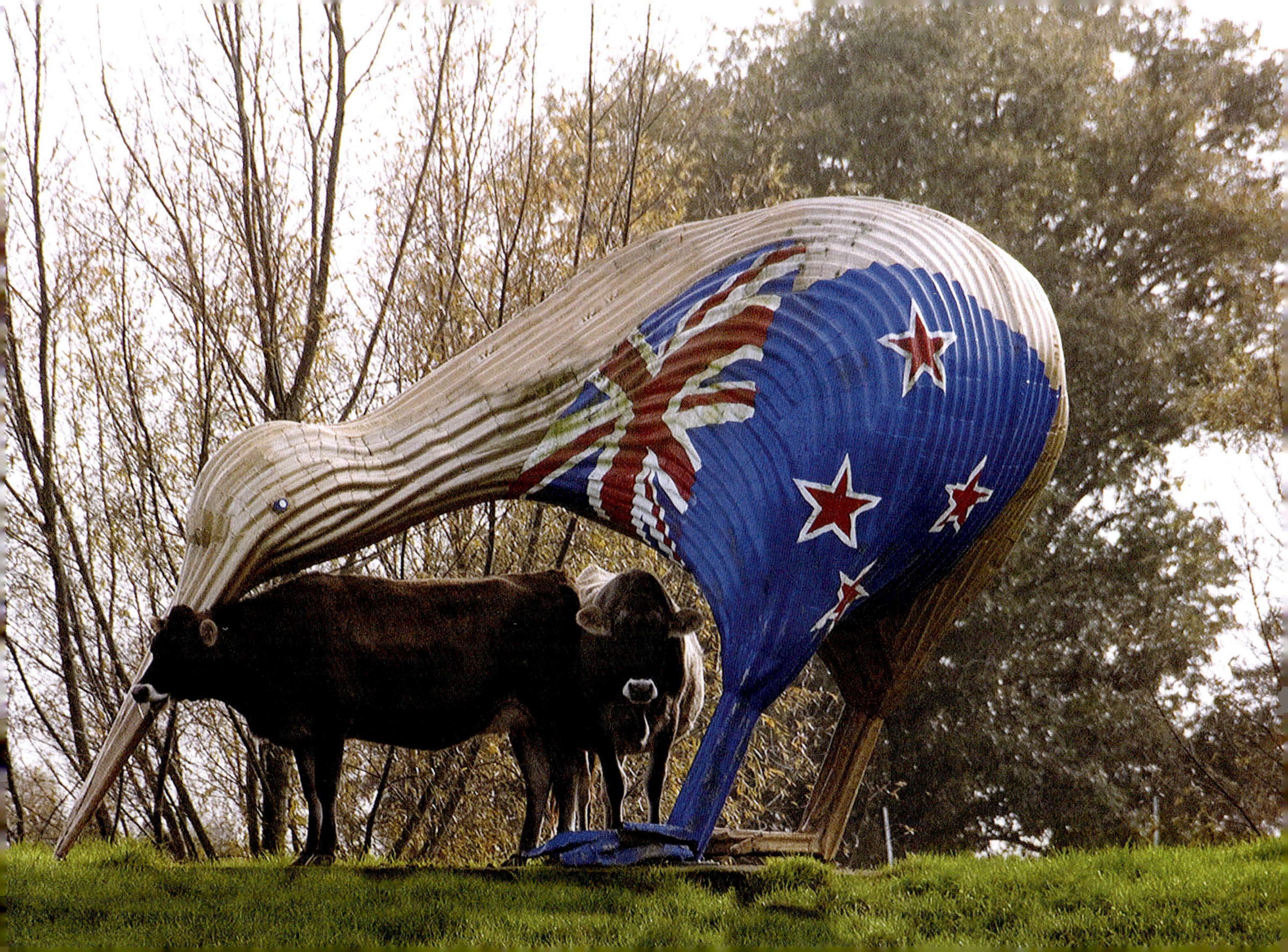

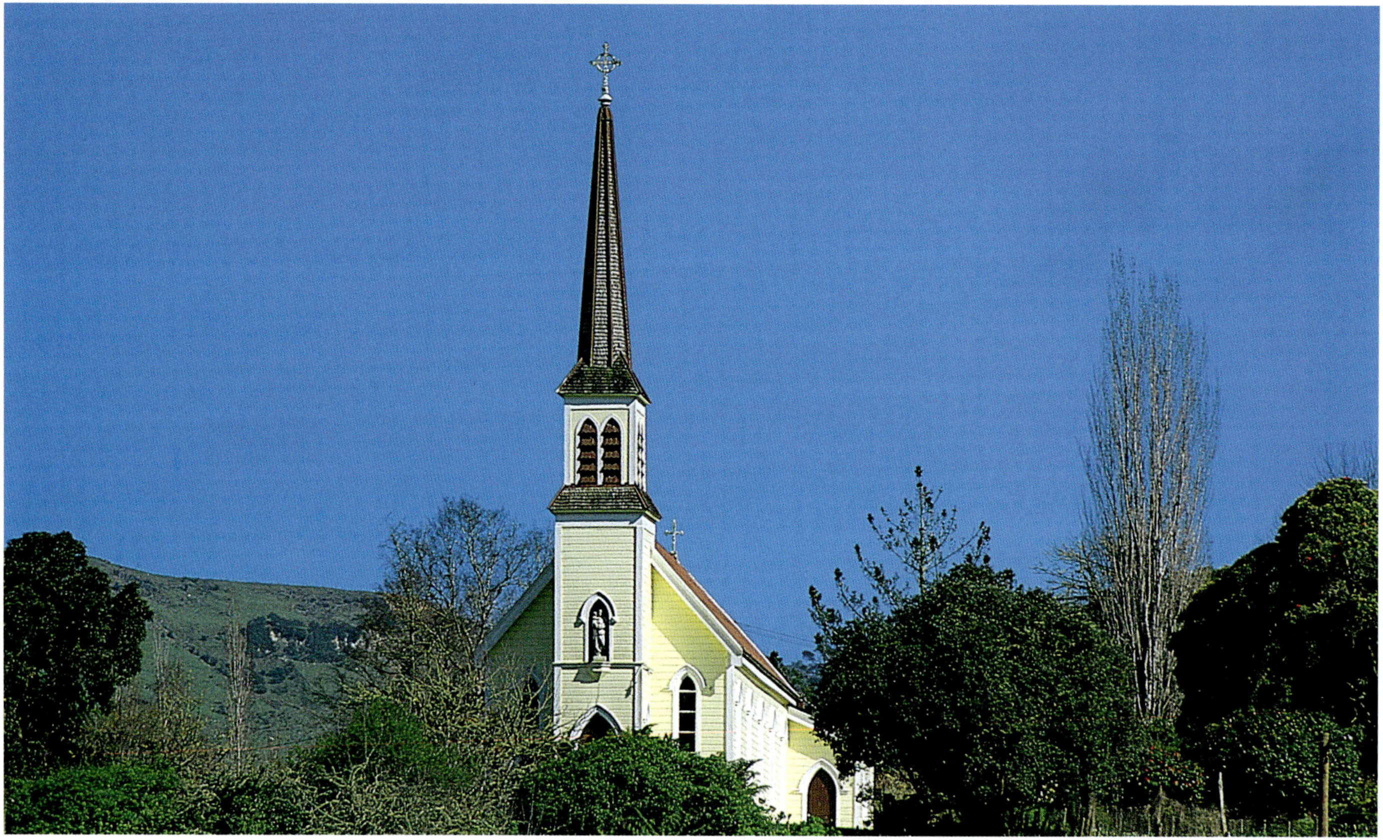

▲ St Joseph's Church at Jerusalem on the Whanganui River, near where poet James K. Baxter founded a commune. Horses ranged free on muddy dirt roads in this area when I had my first-ever professional assignment, to photograph the eight children attending Matawhero School.

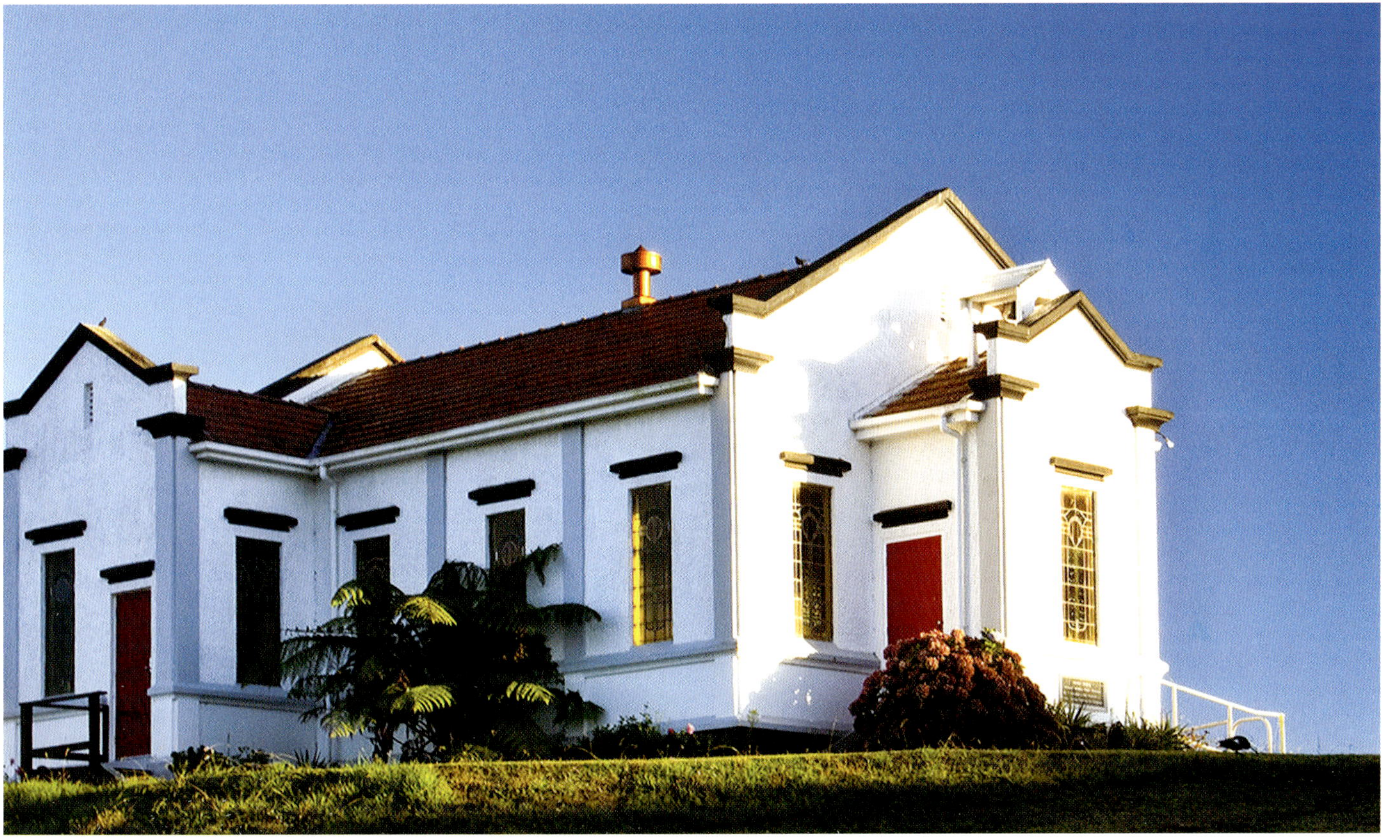

▲ Kawhia Methodist Church lit by sunrise above Kawhia Harbour on the west coast. The great ancestral waka (migratory canoe) Tainui is said to lie buried on the foreshore nearby.

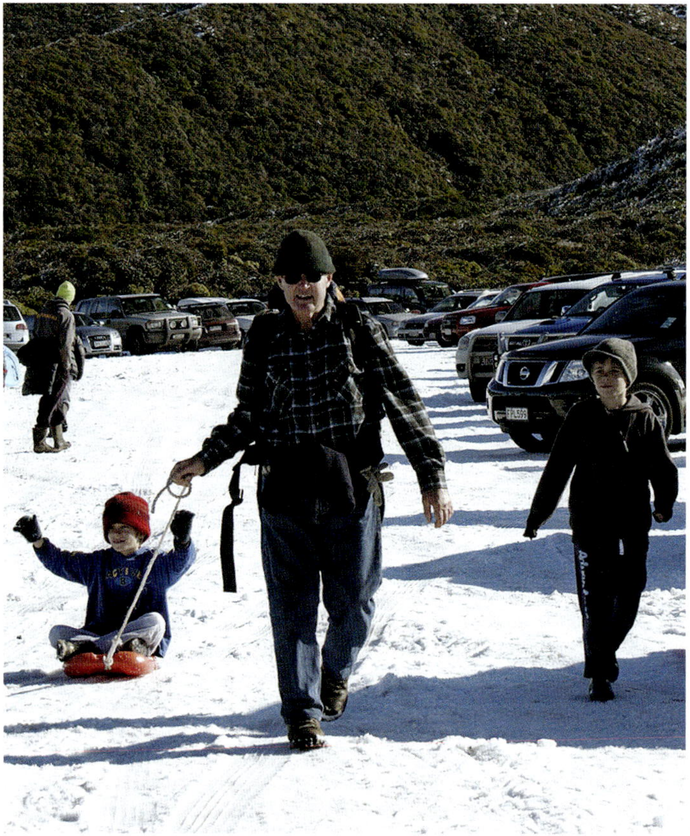

▲ You'll find plenty of winter thrills – with easy access for young and old – at the ski field close to Stratford Mountain House on Mount Taranaki.

▶ Late afternoon light and a front-seat view combine to deliver a unique perspective of Tongariro National Park's mountain peaks and thermal lakes.

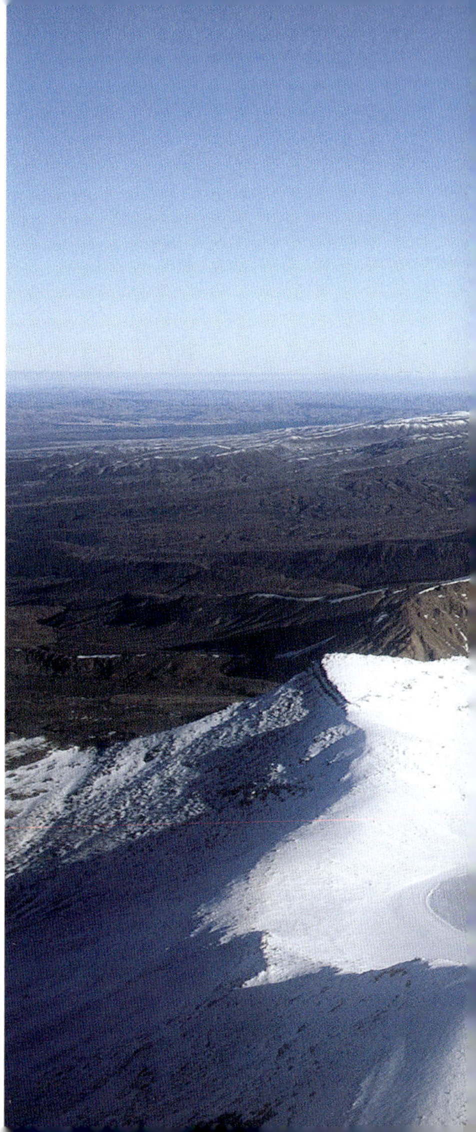

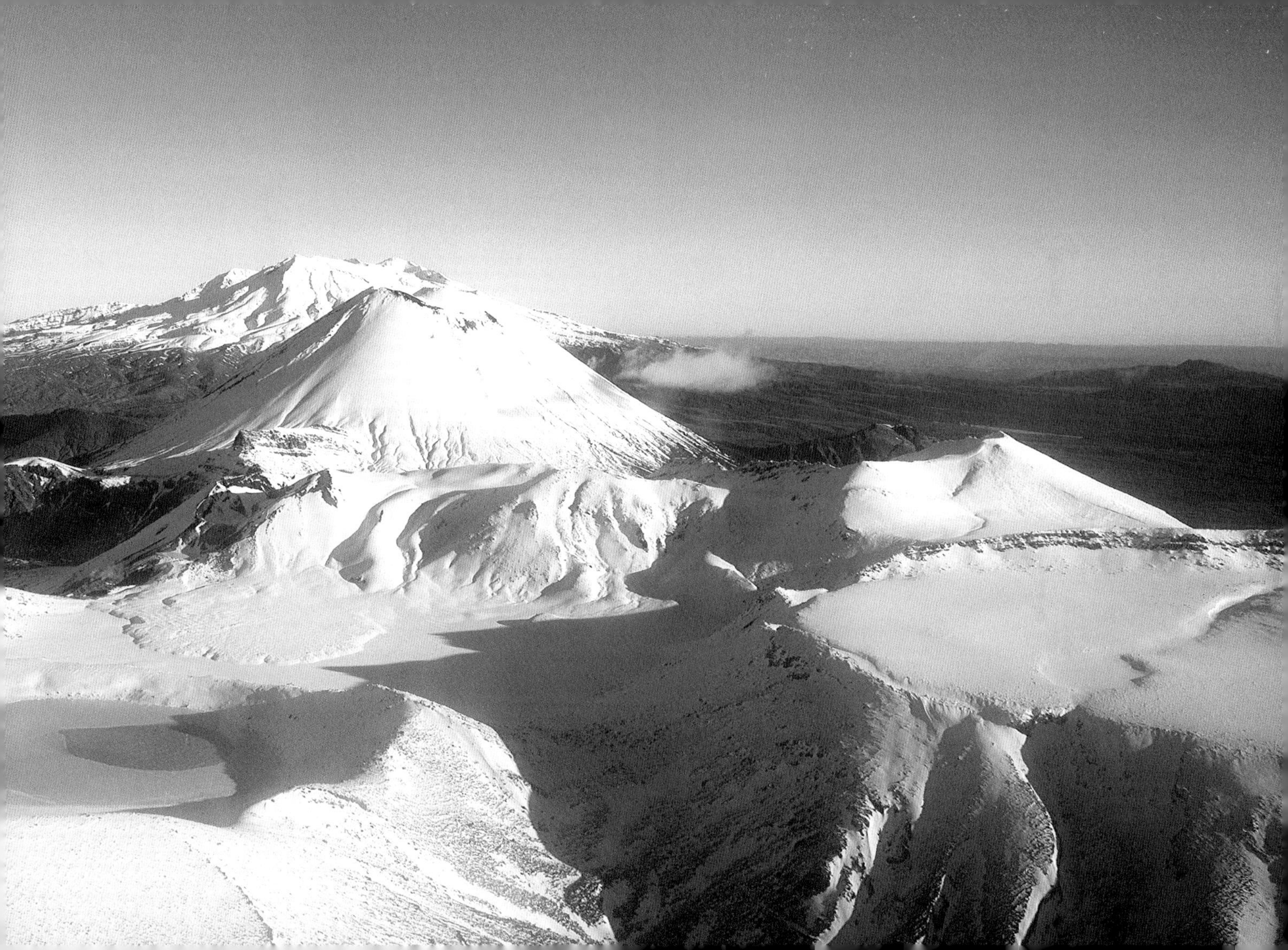

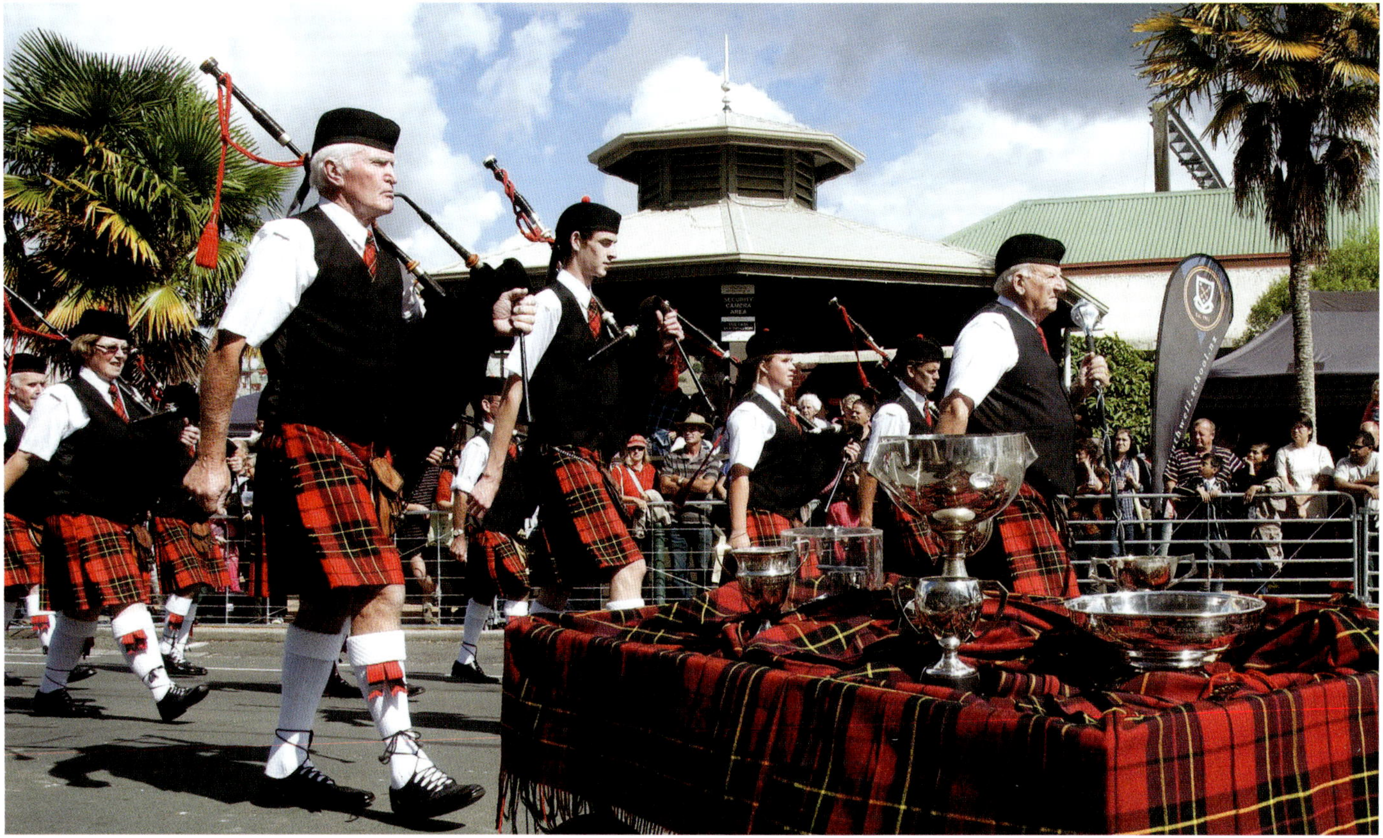

▲ The Te Kuiti & District pipe band leads the Running of the Sheep parade, during which 1000 sheep are let loose to race down the street.

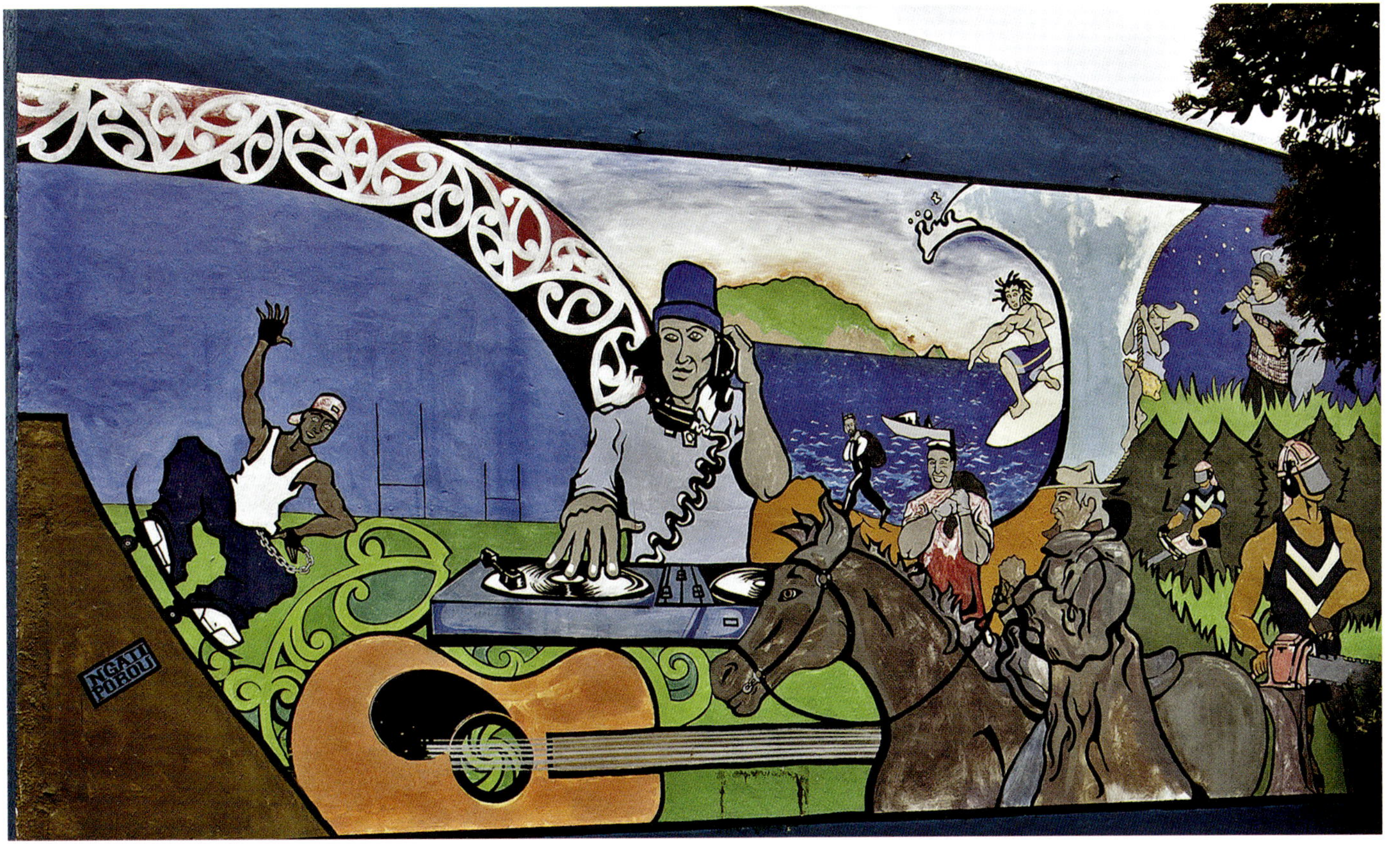

▲ Ruatoria's Ngati Porou (the local Maori tribe) mural defines the rich culture and colour of life on the East Coast, in the lee of Mount Hikurangi.

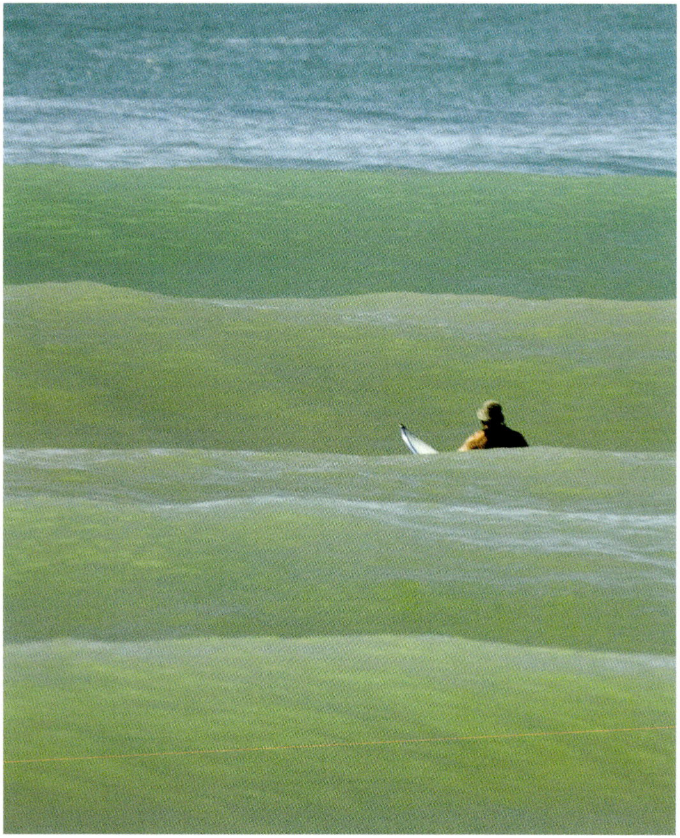

▲ East Coast Highway 35. Roadside surf breaks crest and roll to shore on the journey south to Gisborne.

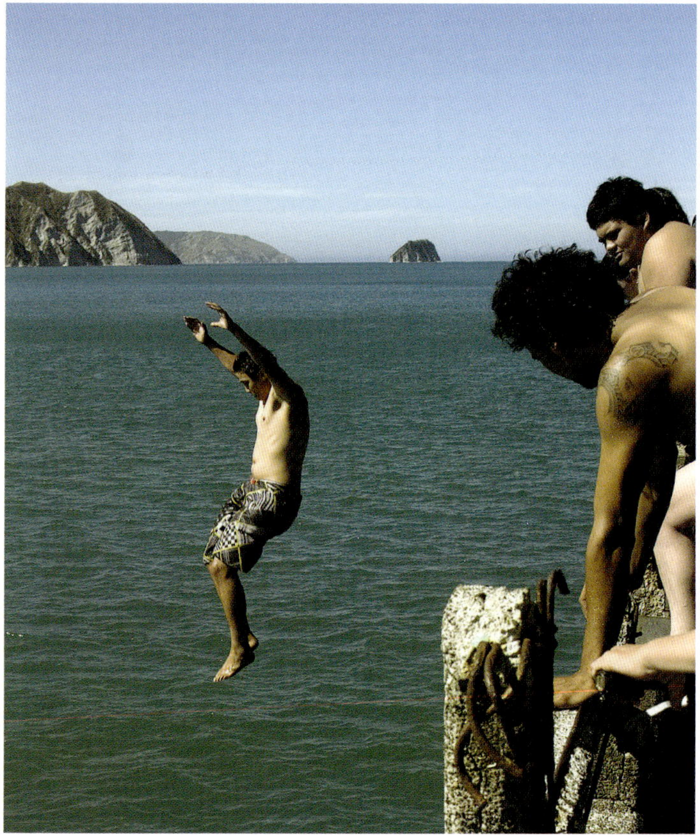

▲ Local lads leap off Tolaga Bay's famous long wharf, built in 1929 and recently restored.

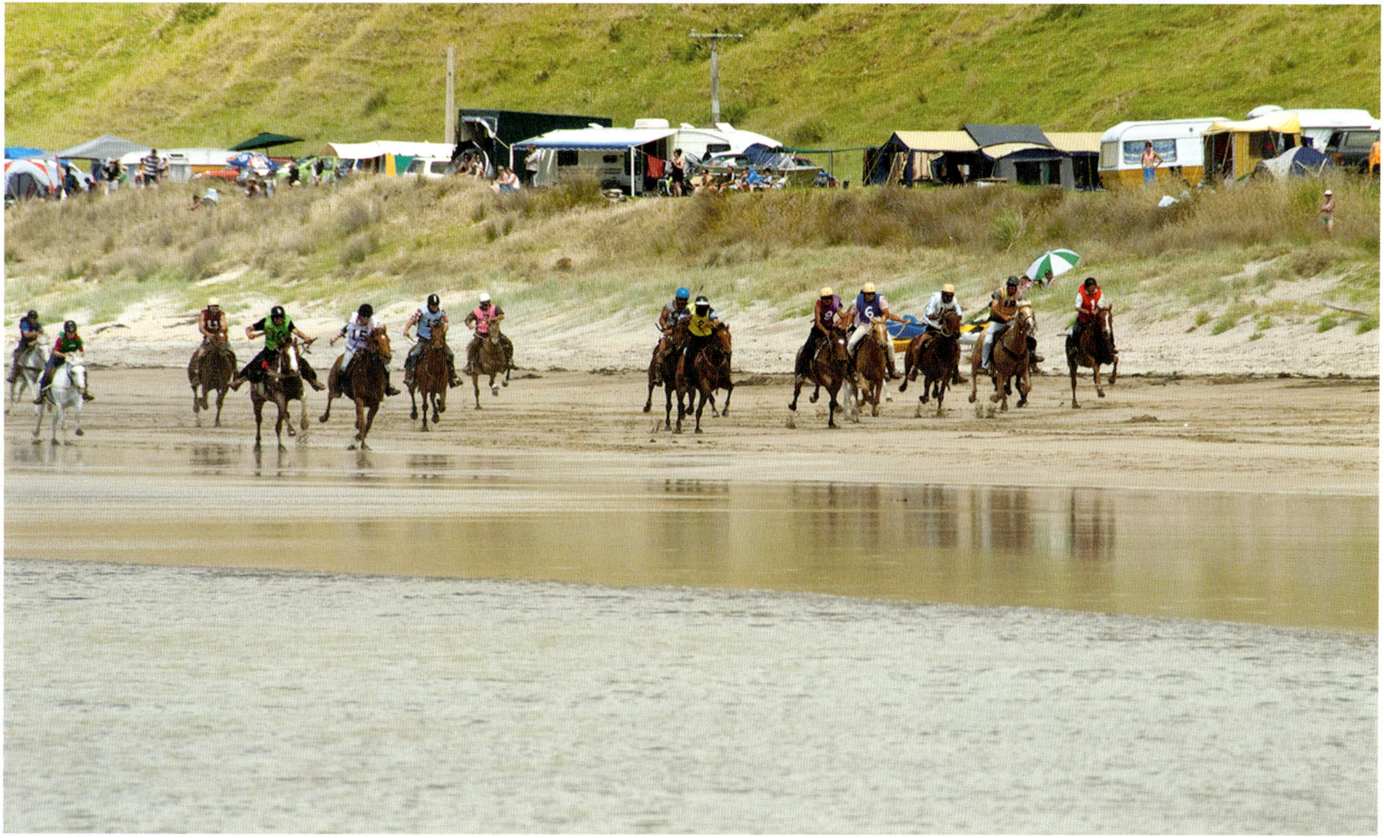

▲ Kaiaua Beach (Tolaga Bay) horse races. The sand vibrates under my feet as the annual race meeting gets underway. Inspiring them all is 78-year-old grandmother, Dinah Atkins (in the red jacket on the right) who competes with her whanau (family).

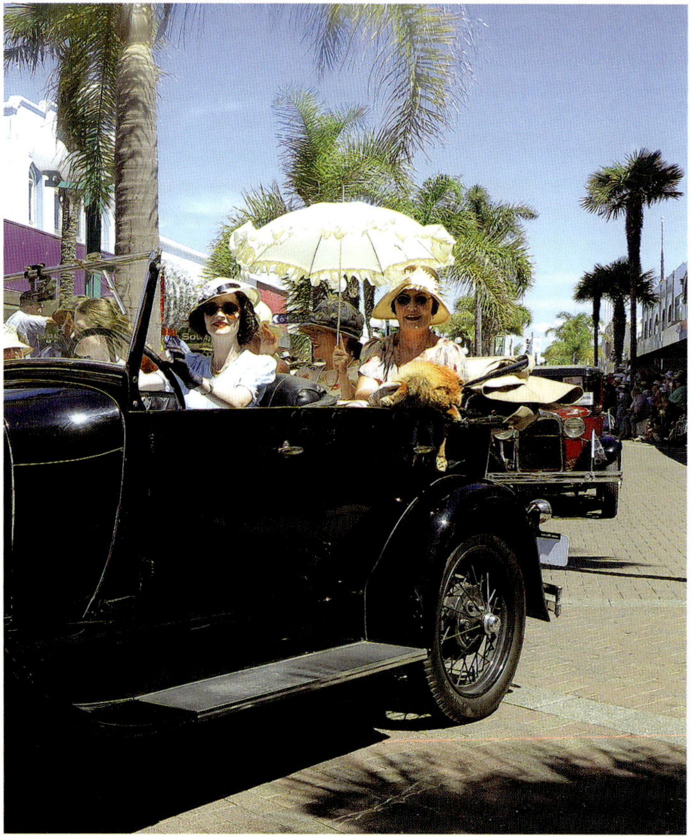

▲ Glamour and fun are the order of the weekend at Napier's annual Art Deco celebrations.

▶ Air Force 'aerobats' dance, airborne with Art Deco rooftop art – or so it seems from down below!

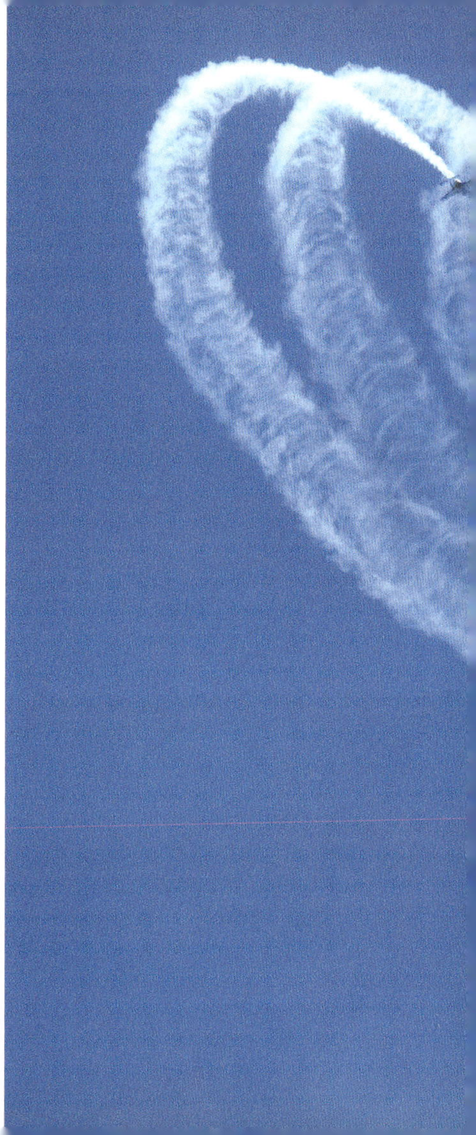

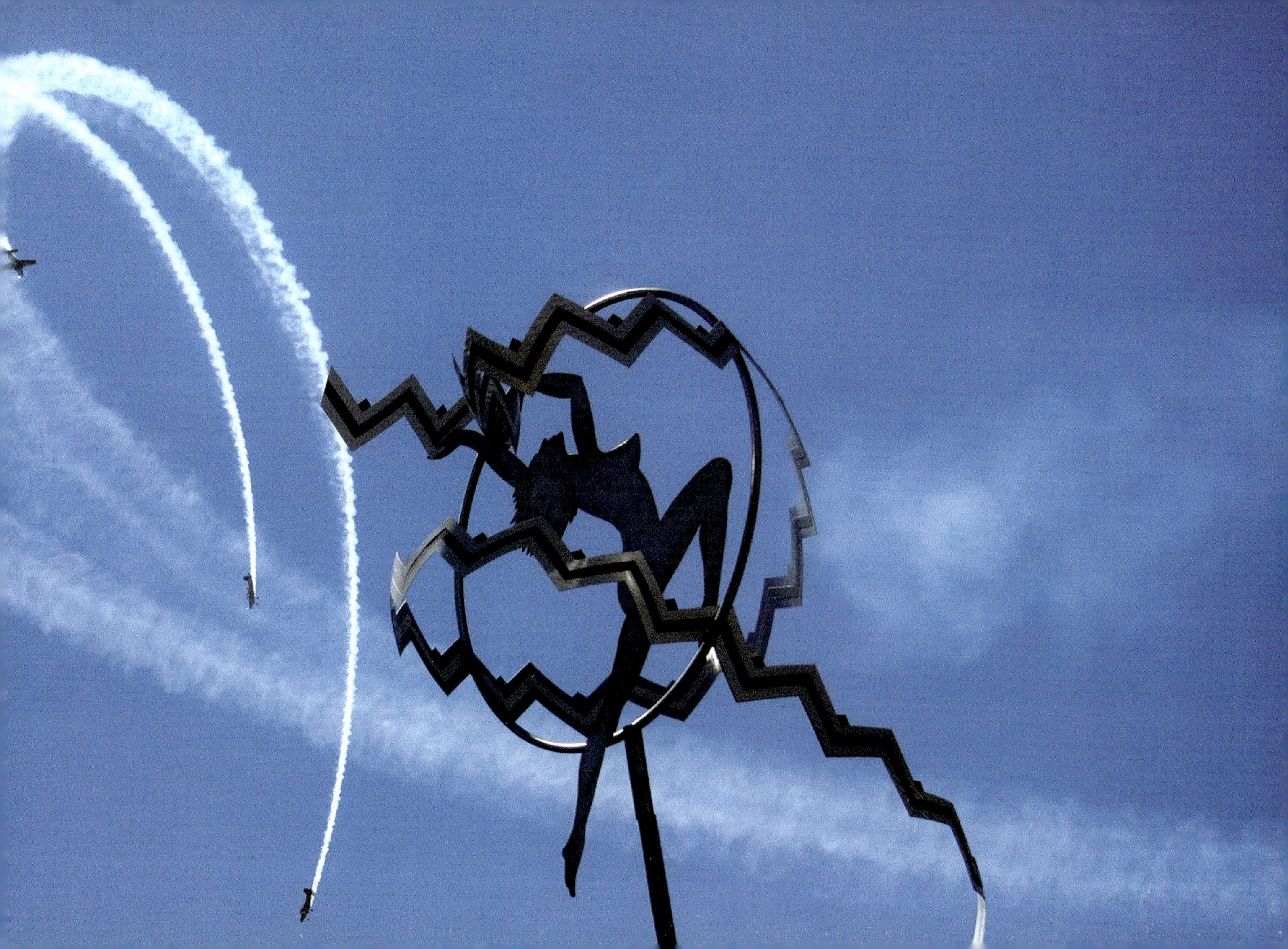

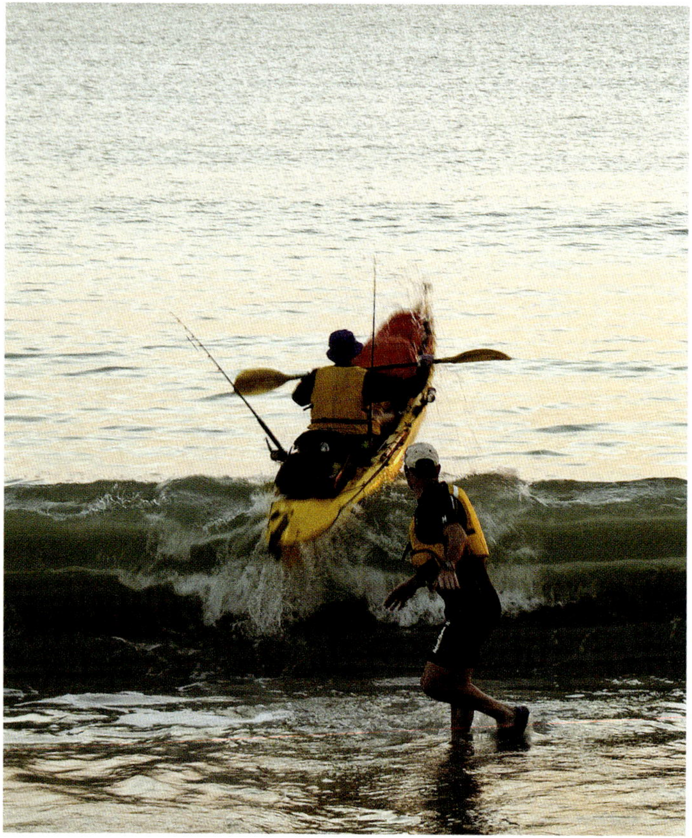

▲ Clifton Beach, Napier. An earlybird fishing expedition gets off to a bumpy start.

▶ The magnificent beach stretches right up to Cape Kidnappers, where nature pulls out all the stops.

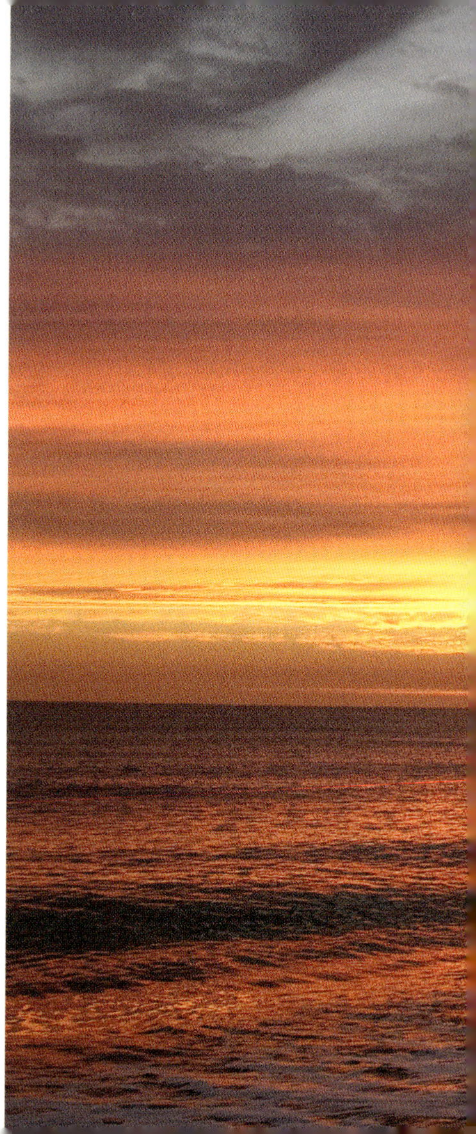

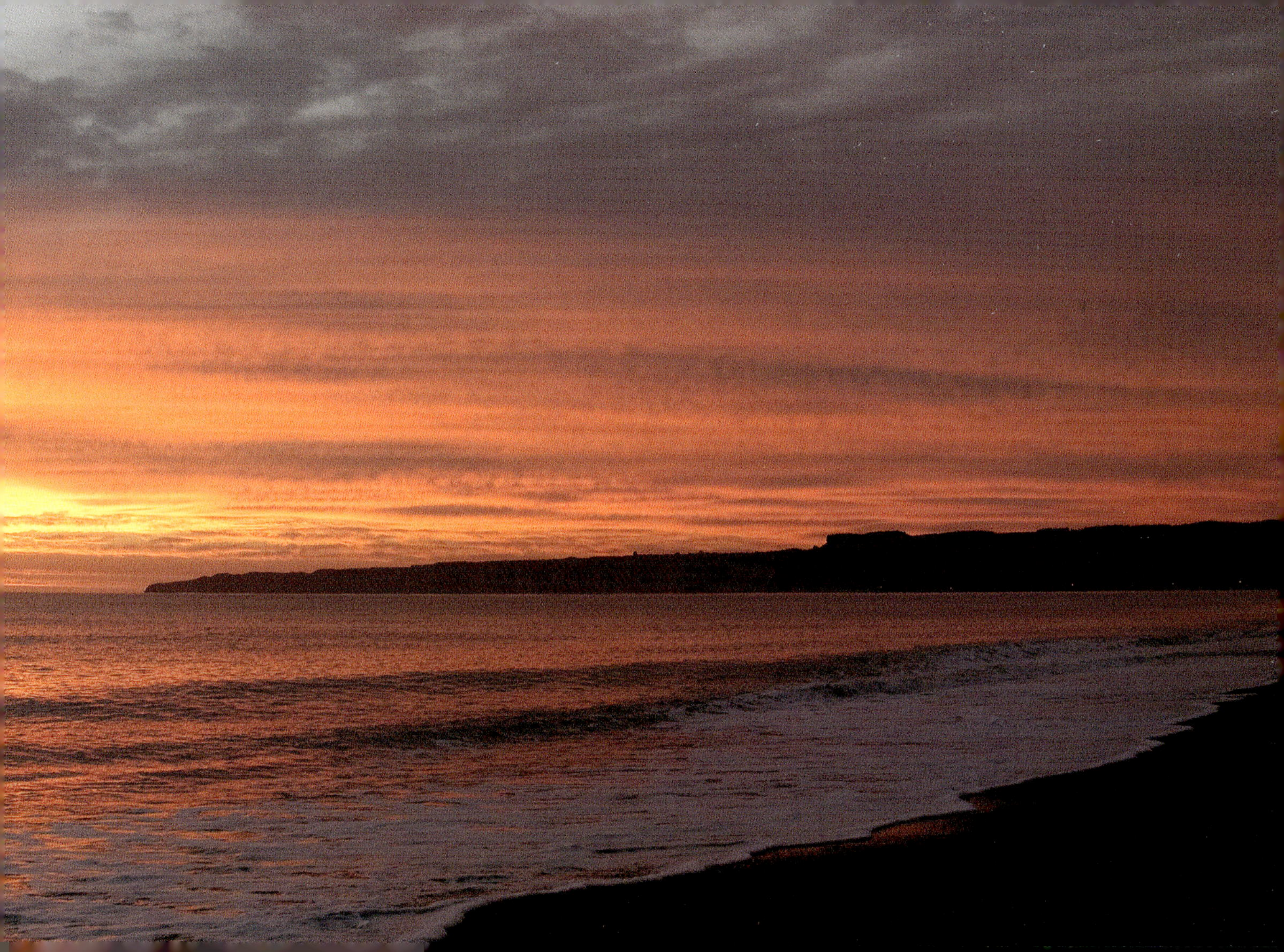

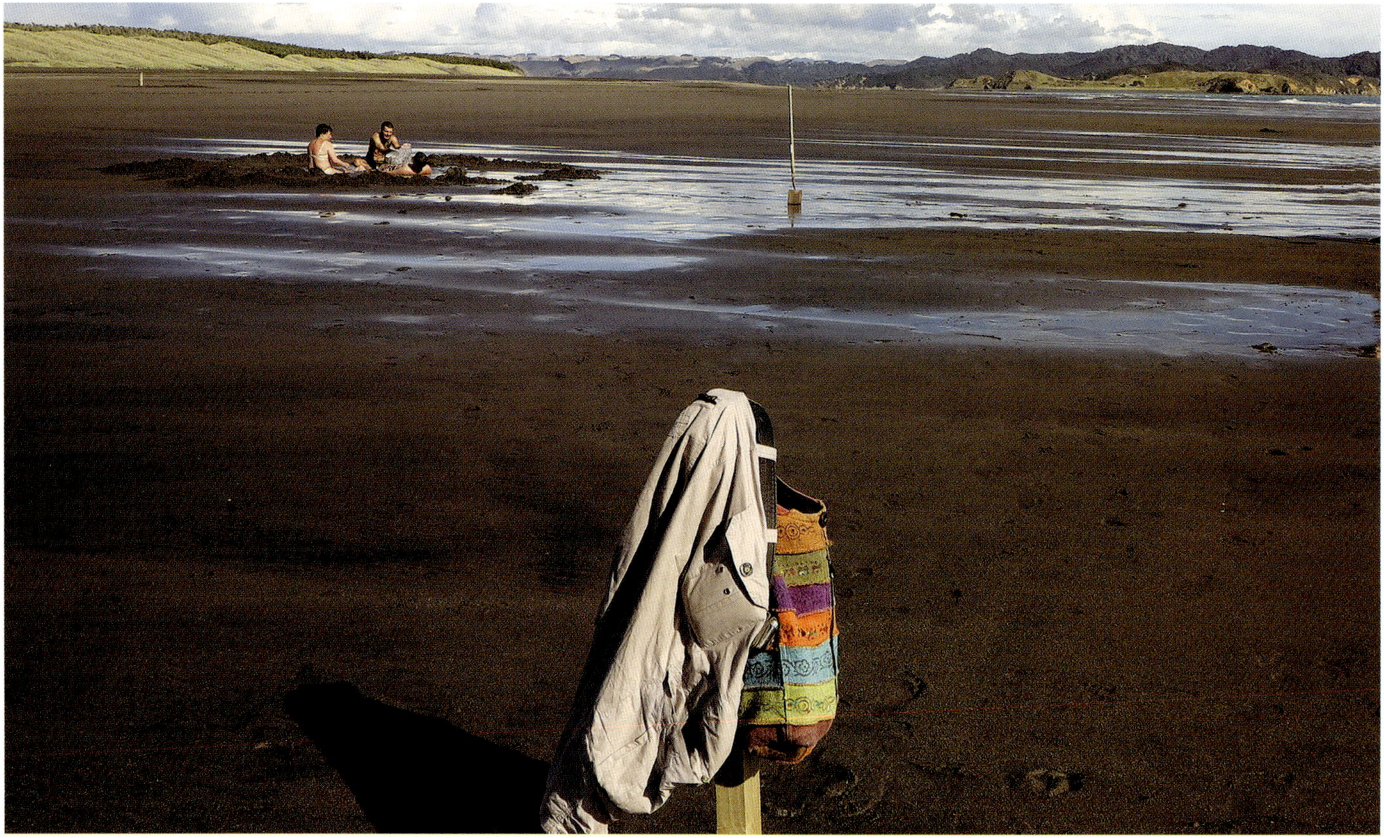

▲ Maukutea Beach at Kawhia where you can enjoy a long soak in the hot geothermal waters that bubble up through the black iron-rich sand.

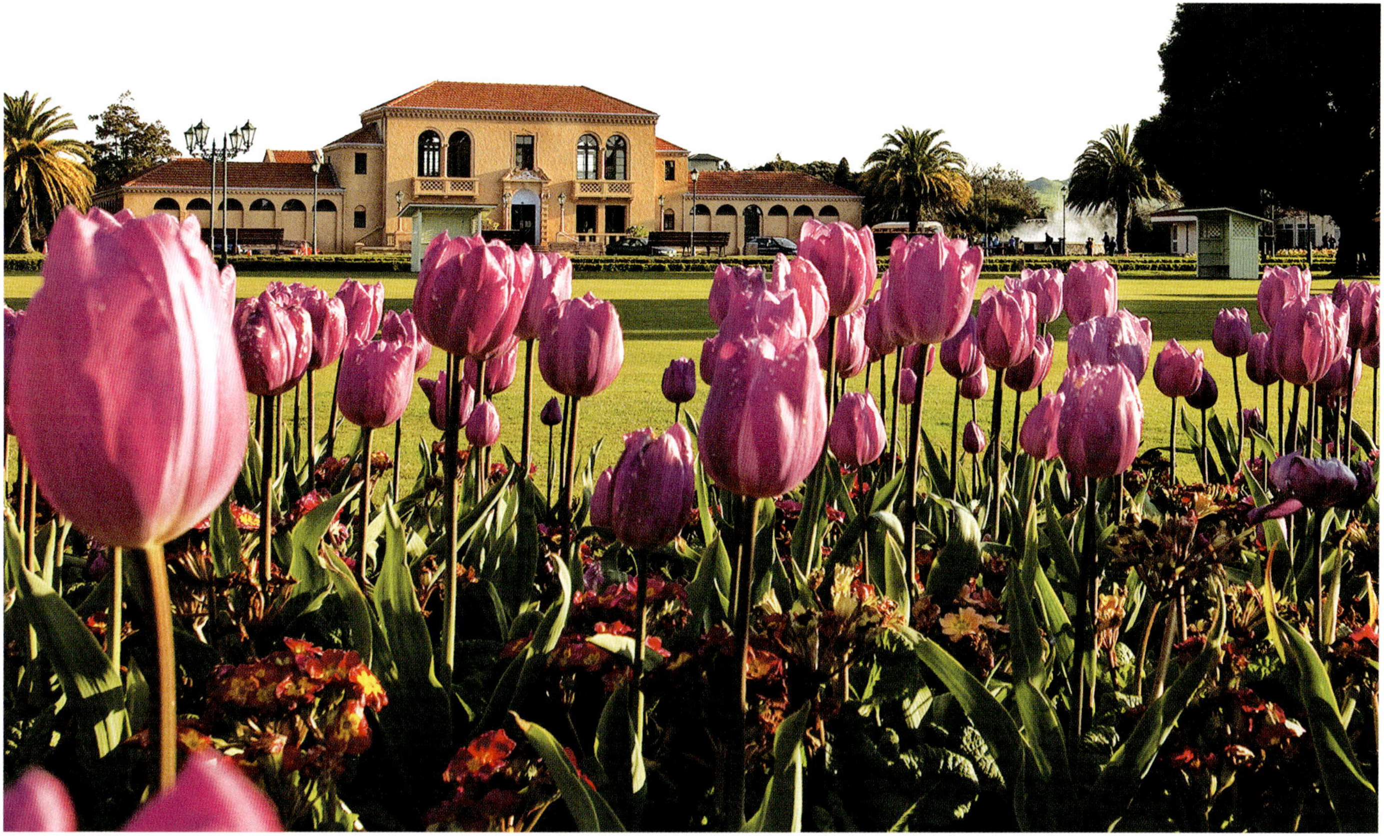

▲ Vibrant tulip beds draw me in to the tranquil surroundings of the historic Blue Baths in Government Gardens, Rotorua.

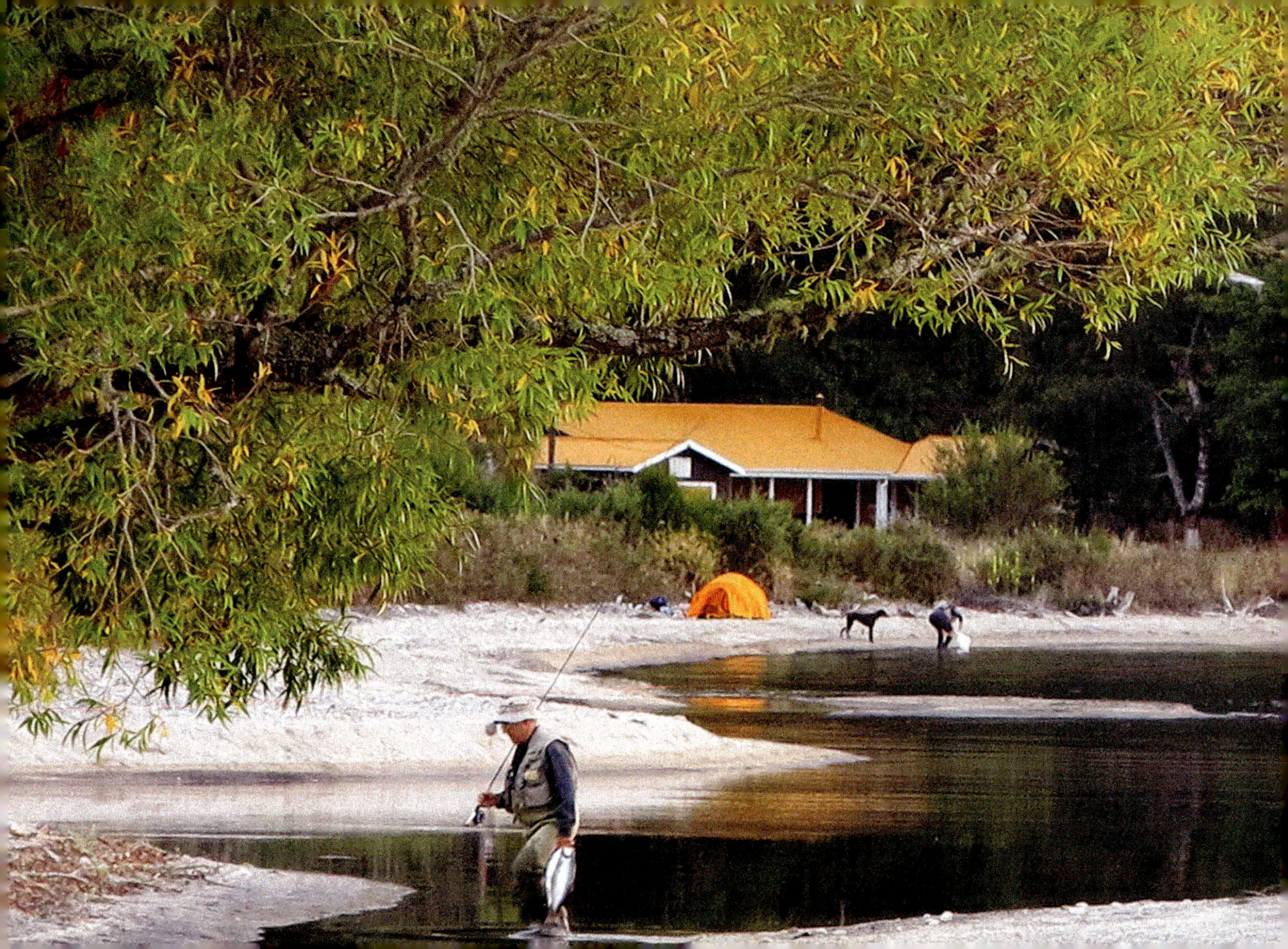

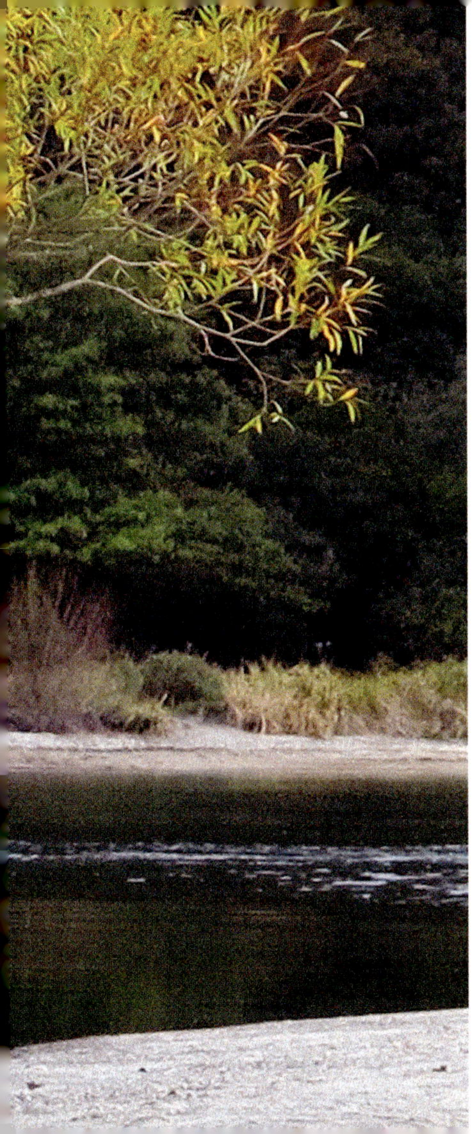

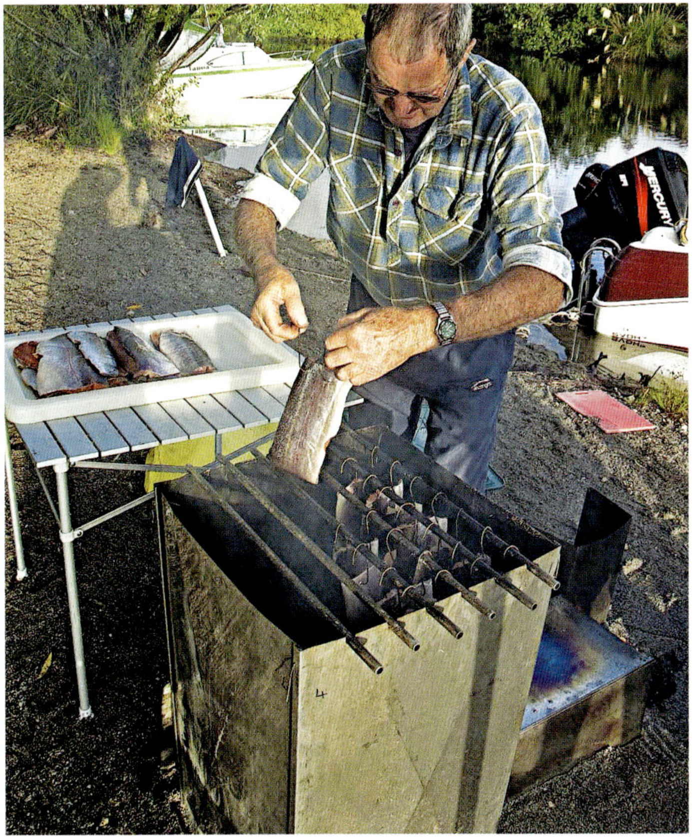

▲ I've watched many rainbow trout smoke-ups and have enjoyed a lifetime supply of this delicacy prepared by my husband Harry, the 'Mayor of Waihaha', as he's known to locals.

◀ The Waihaha rip gives up another rainbow trout on the shores of Lake Taupo.

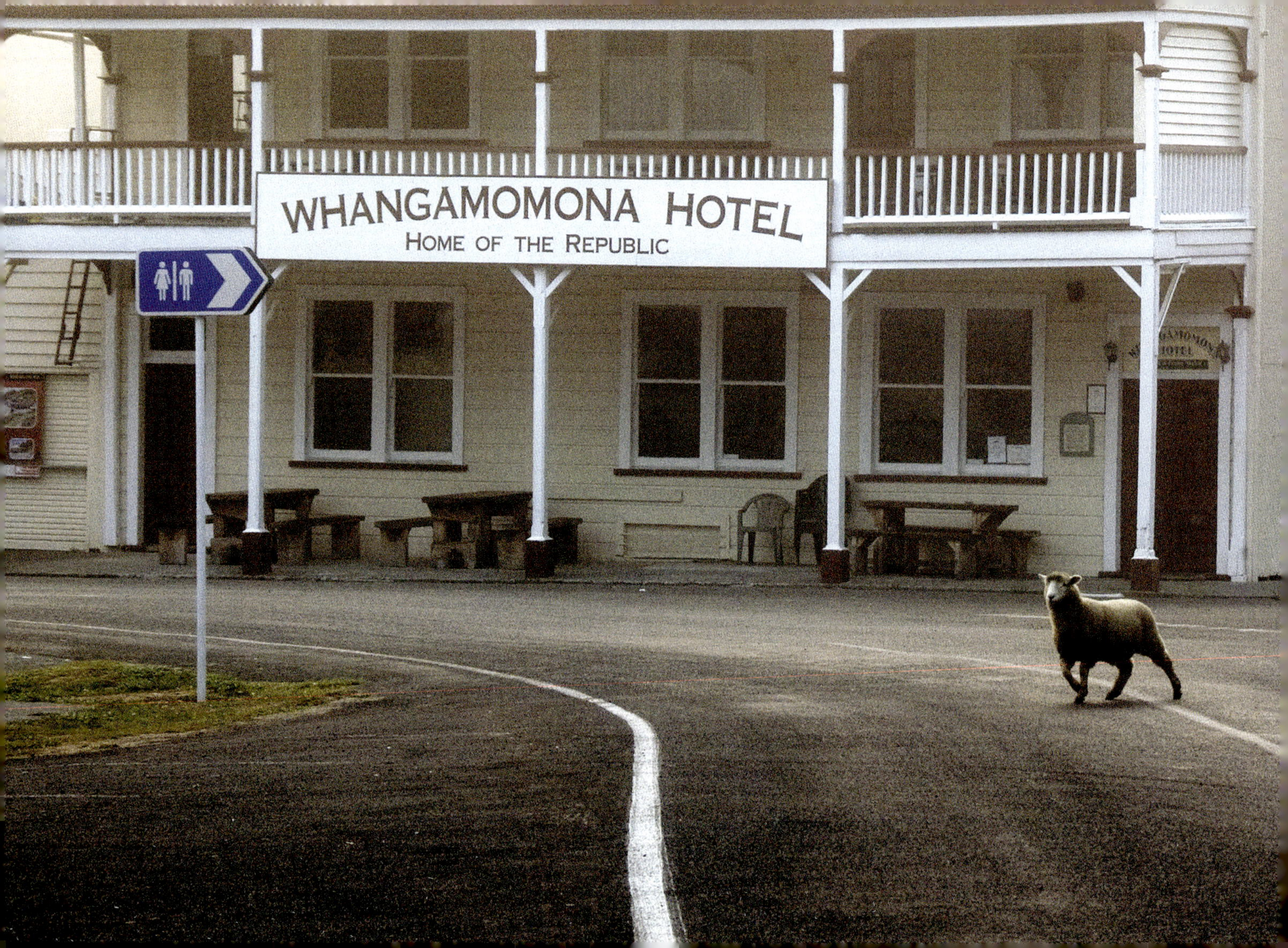
WHANGAMOMONA HOTEL
HOME OF THE REPUBLIC

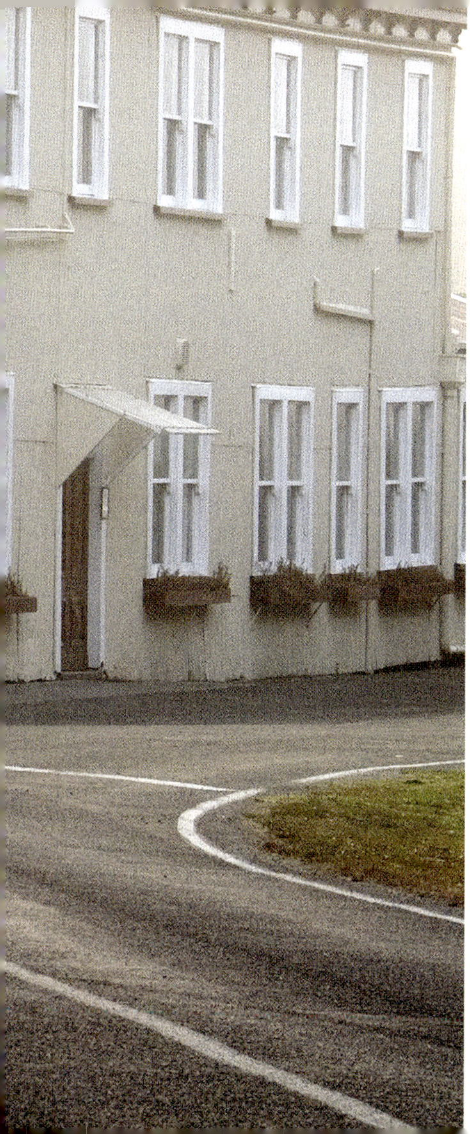

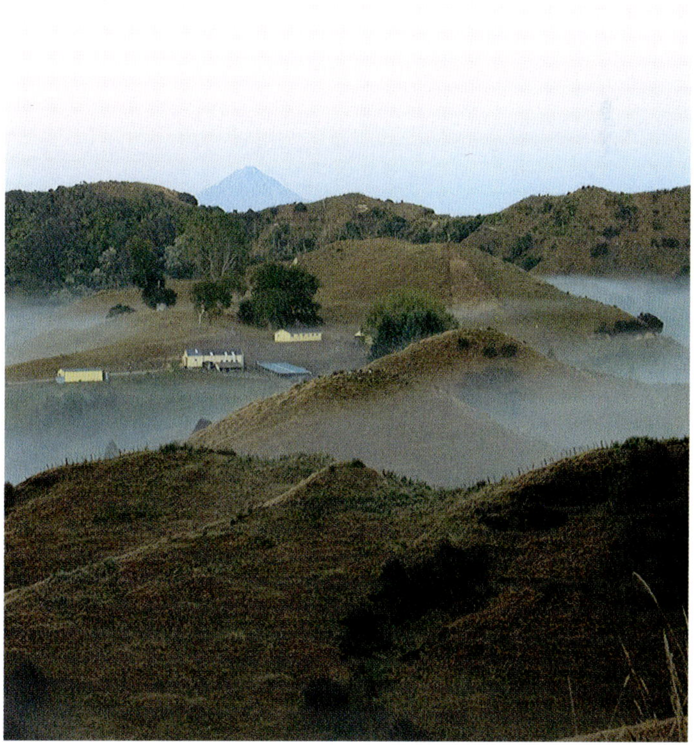

▲ Looking ghostly in the mist, Mount Taranaki guides travellers along the Forgotten World Highway.

◀ There's just me and a solitary sheep outside the Whangamomona Hotel at daybreak.

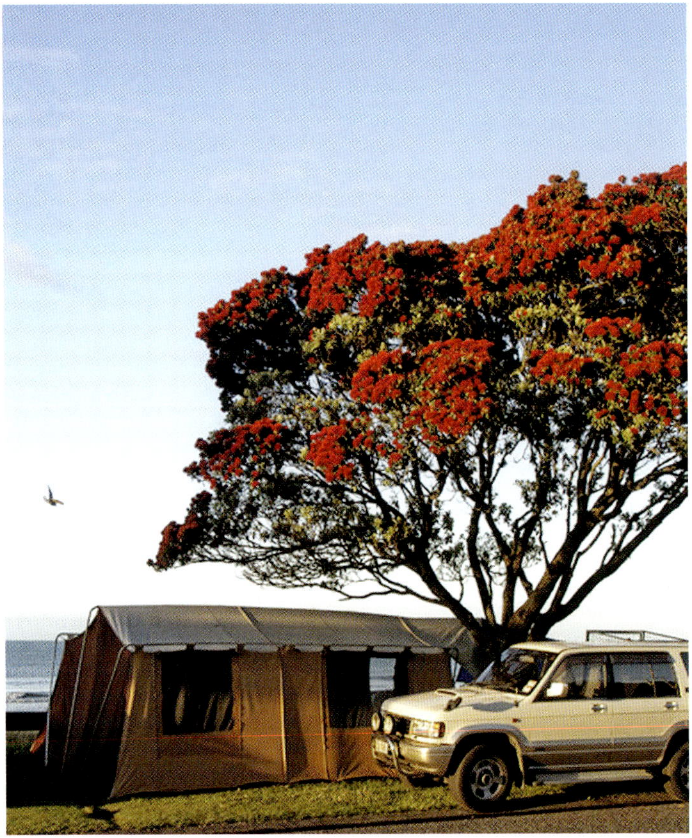

▲ The Oakura Beach Holiday Park in Taranaki with its built-in pohutukawa decor is just a step from the sea.

▶ New Plymouth's Sugar Loaf Islands frame Oakura Beach, a very special surf beach – not least because it's my stamping ground.

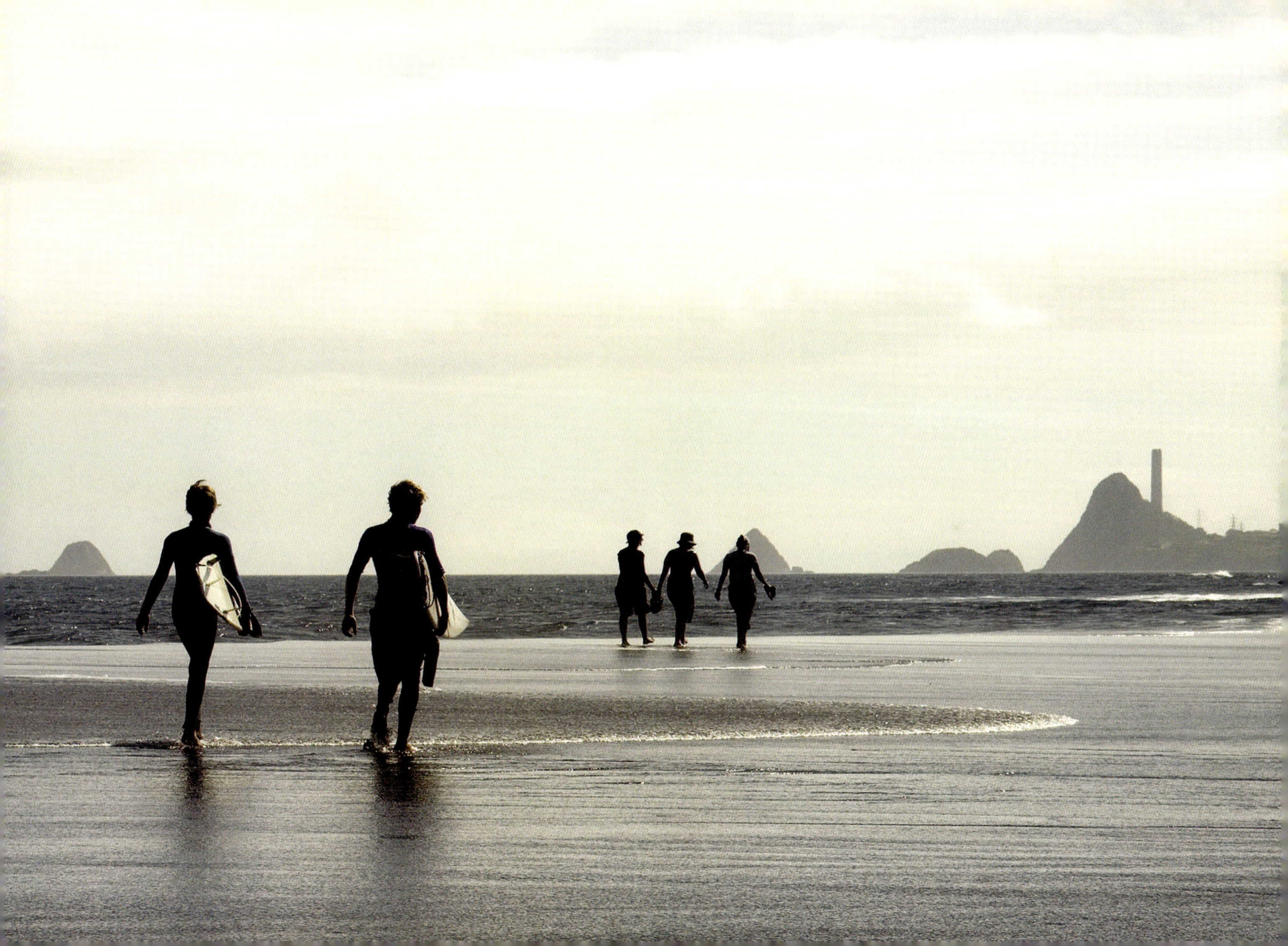

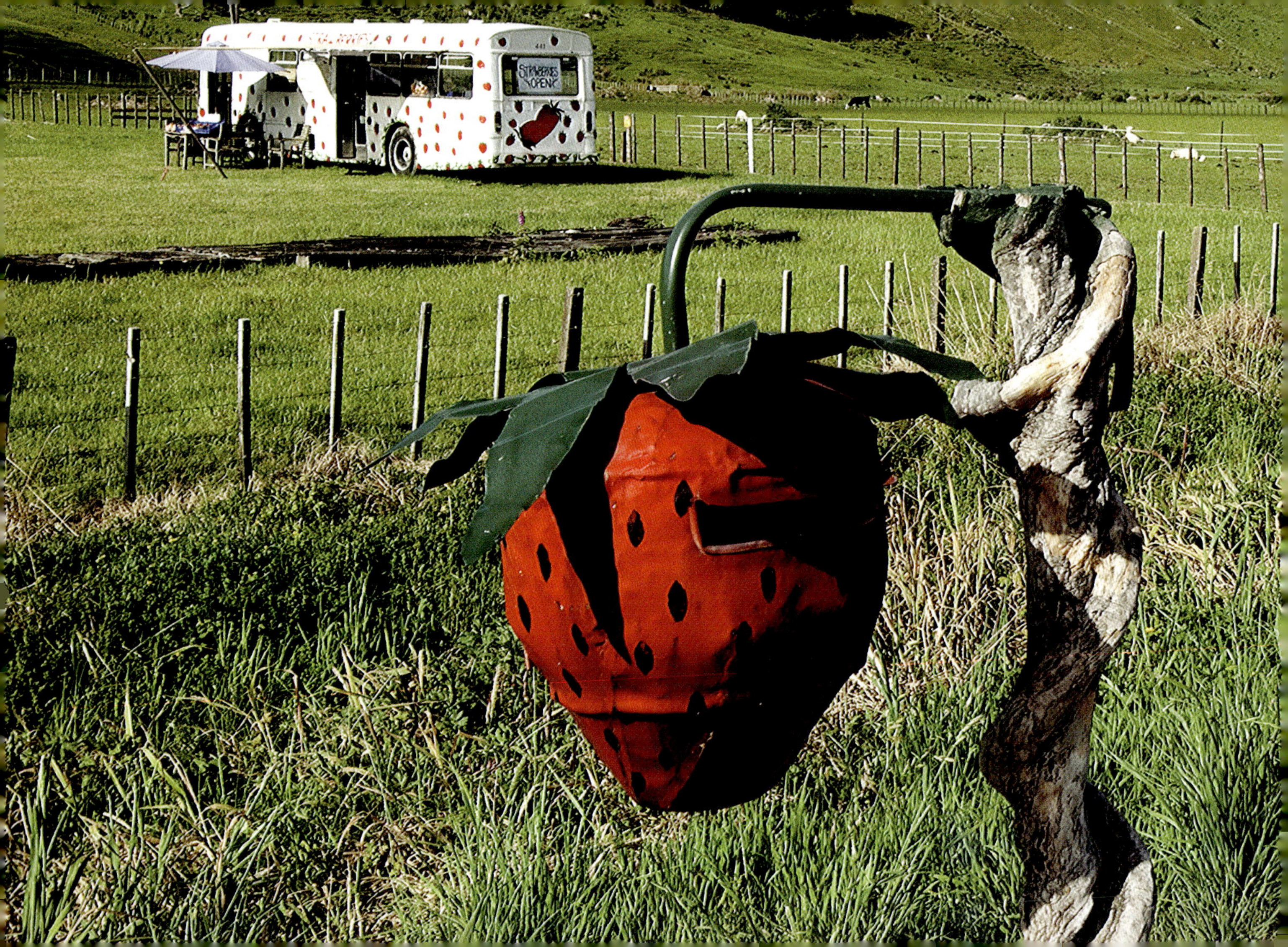
OPEN

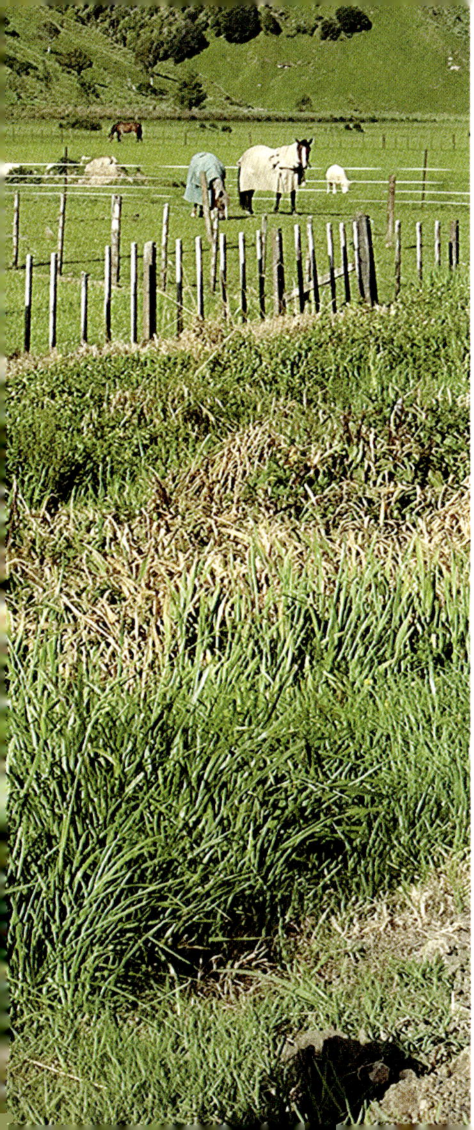

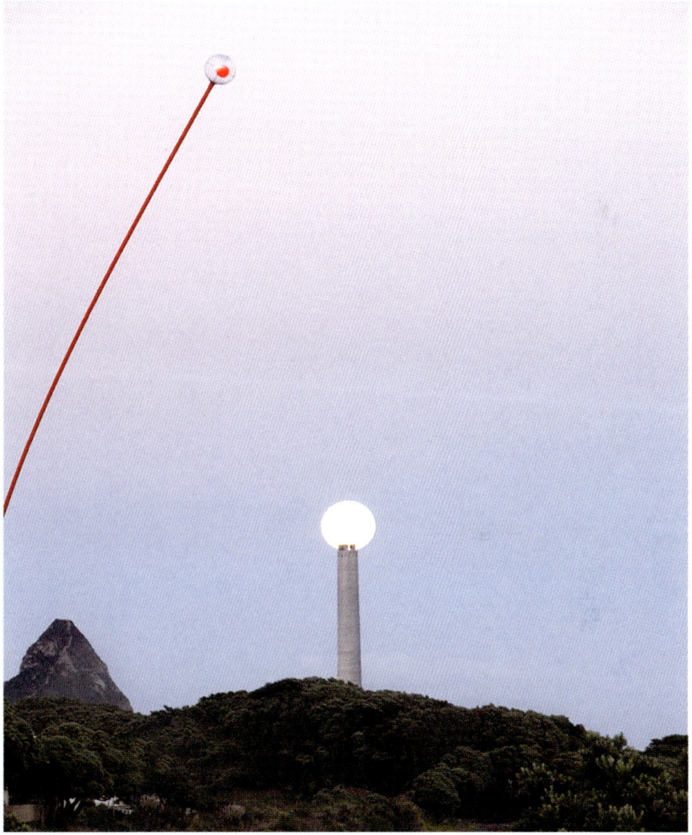

▲ The great smoke stack of New Plymouth Power Station appears to support a full moon while Len Lye's kinetic Wind Wand bends down for a closer look.

◀ A strawberry letterbox leads to a strawberry bus – and real strawberries too, when they're in season – near Awakino on Highway 45.

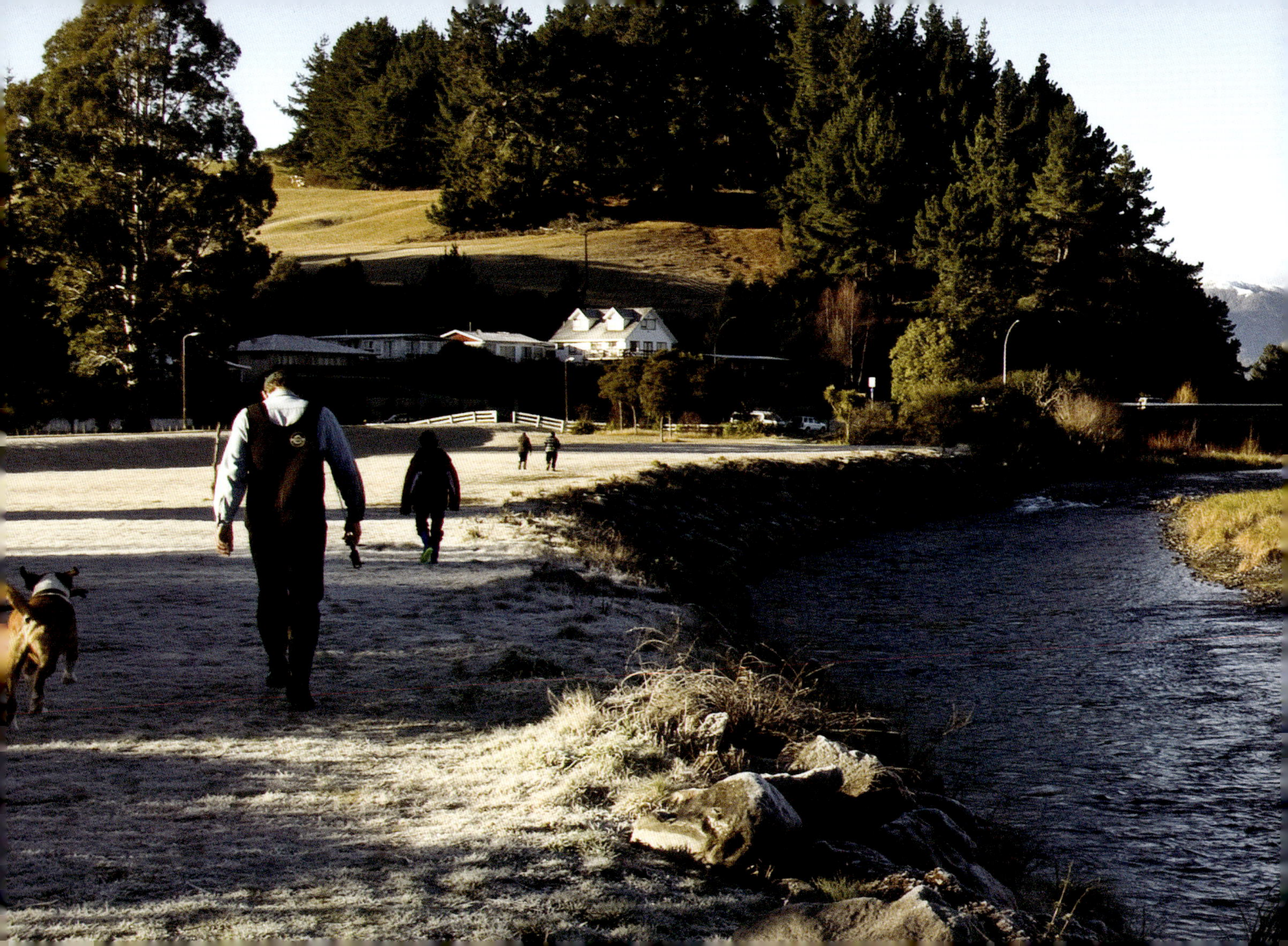

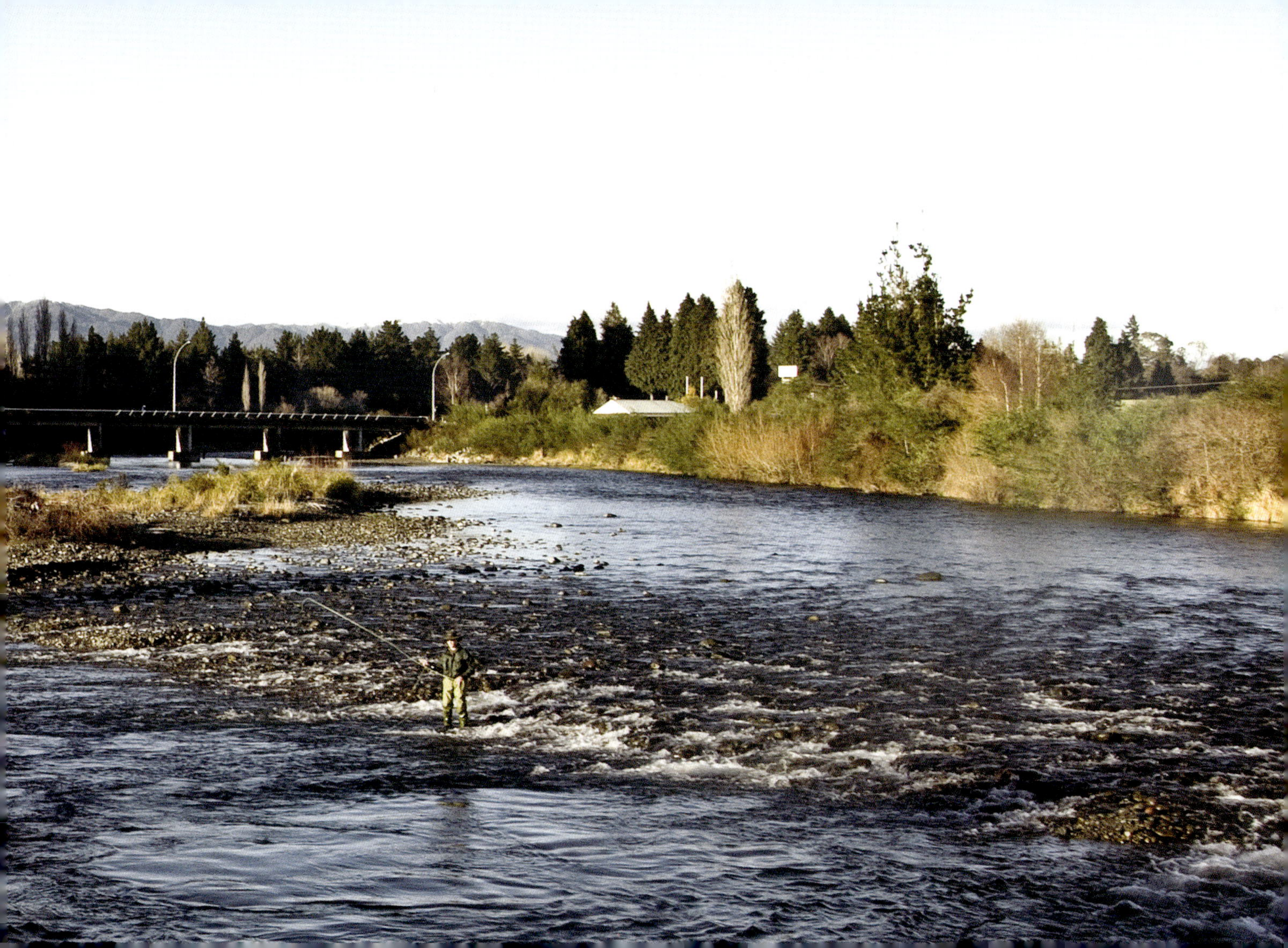

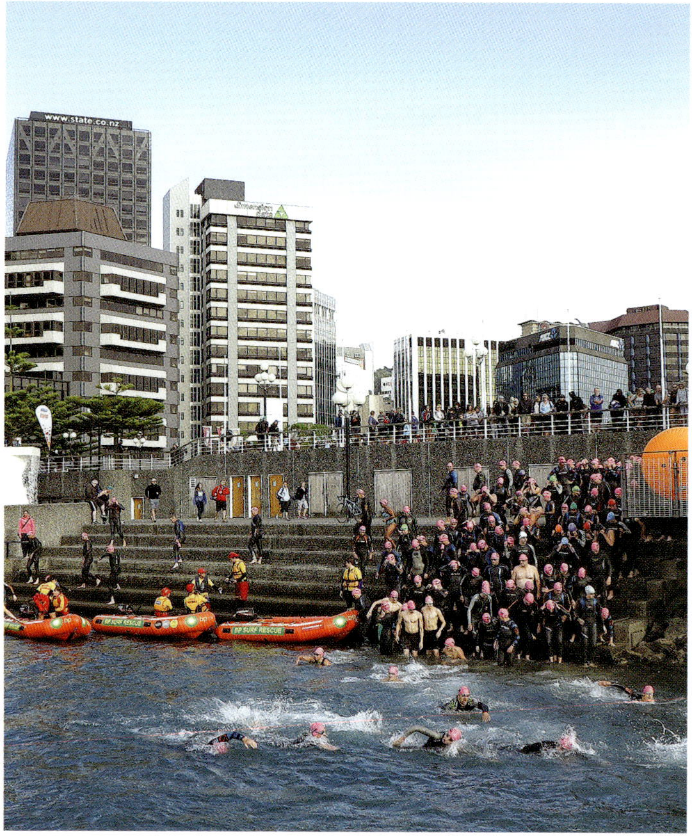

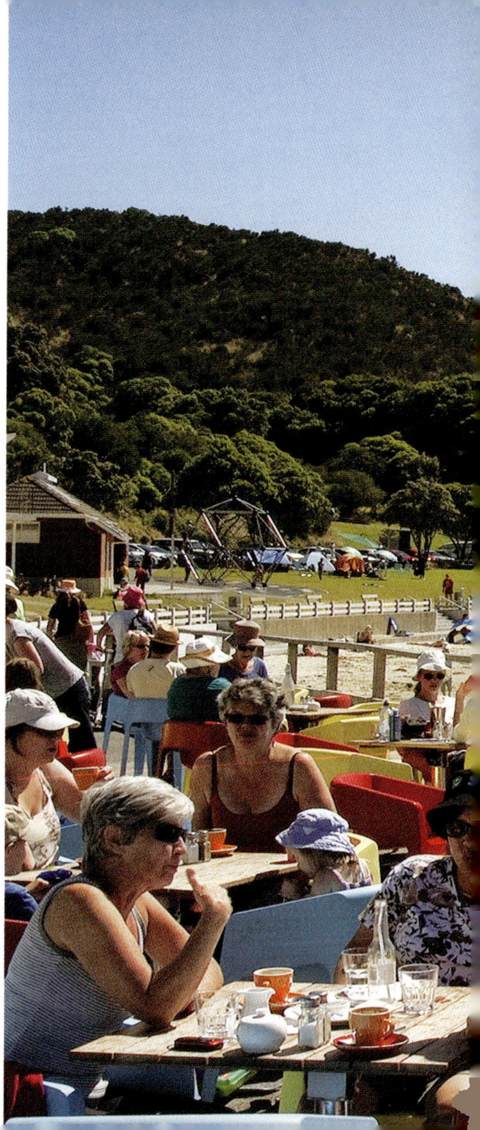

▲ An avalanche of swimmers pours into Wellington Harbour for the annual State Ocean Swim Series.

▶ A perfect Wellington day at Scorch-O-Rama café, Scorching Bay.

◀◀ The Tongariro River Walkway at Turangi – a mecca for fly fishers.

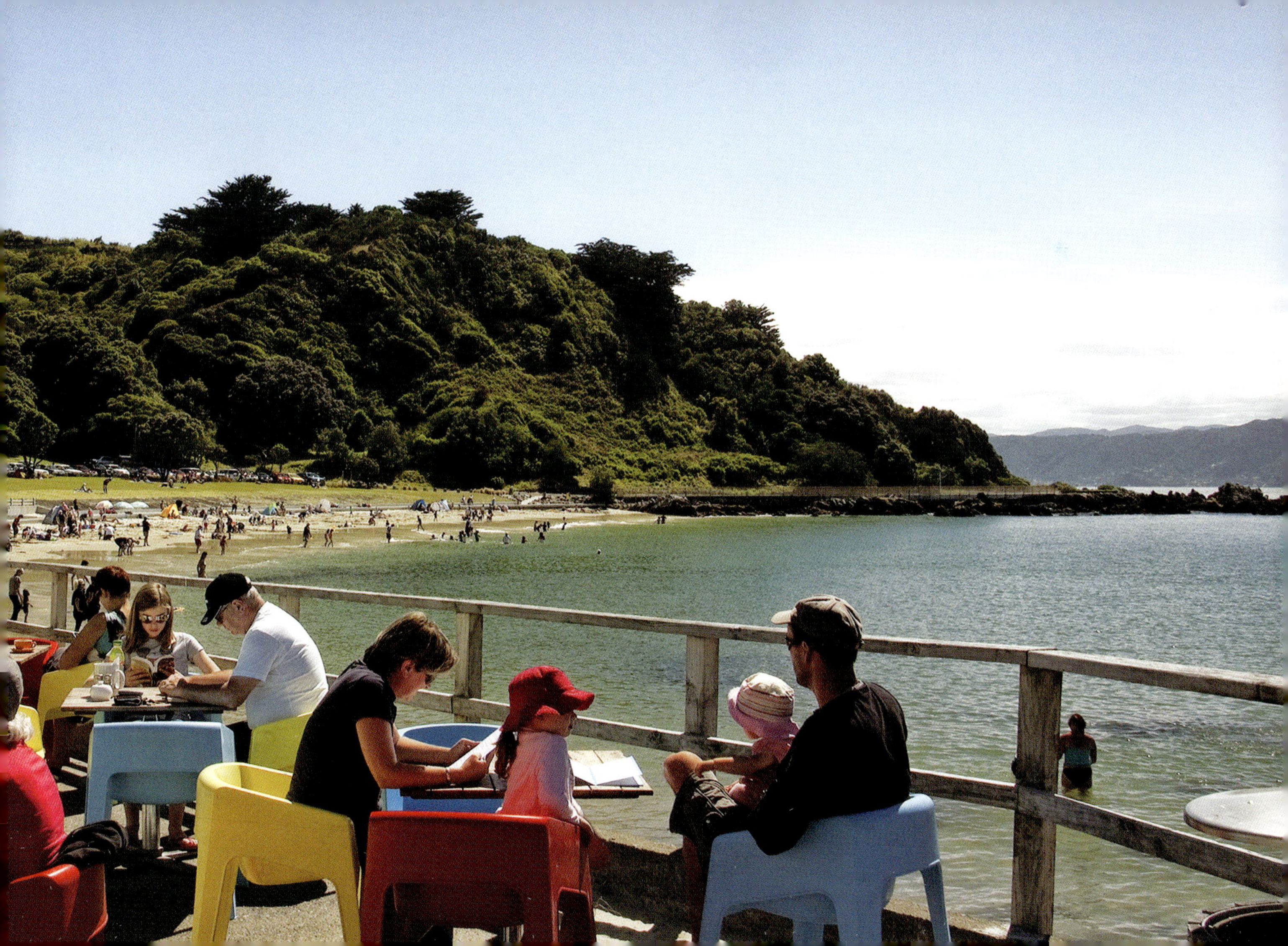

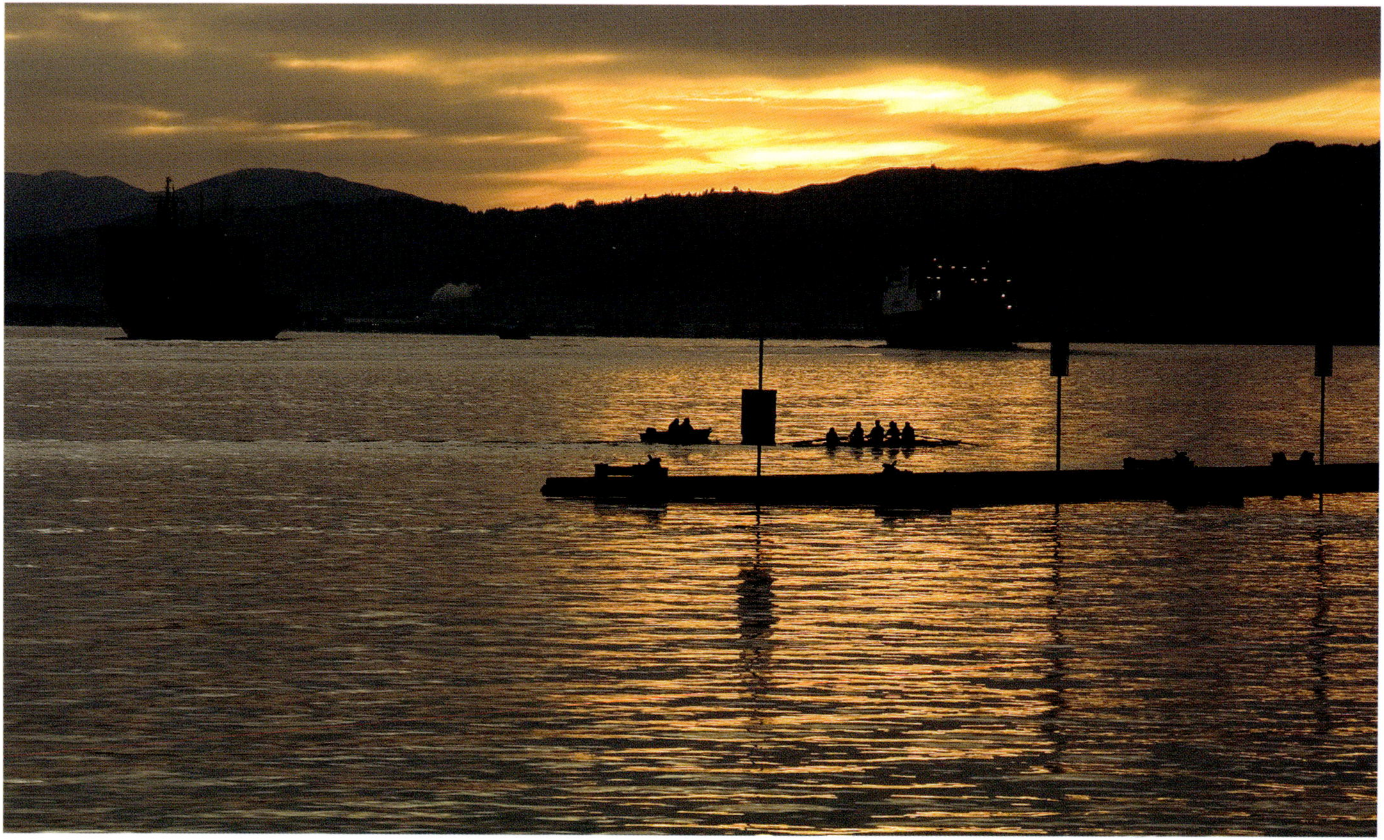

▲ Some keen rowers share the dawn light on Wellington Harbour with me.

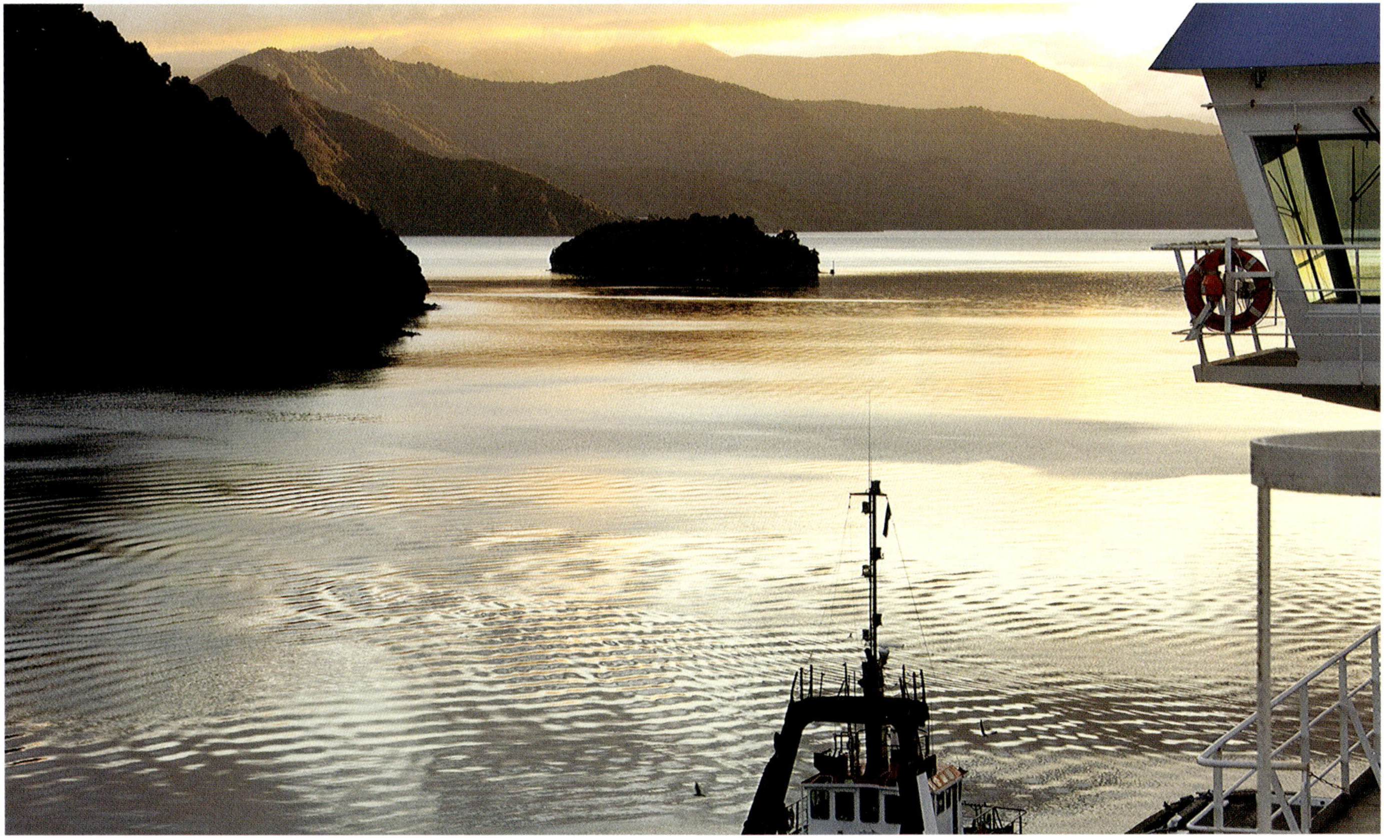

▲ From the deck of the Bluebridge Ferry on its way to Picton, the wake appears to be cast in cut-glass light and shadow.

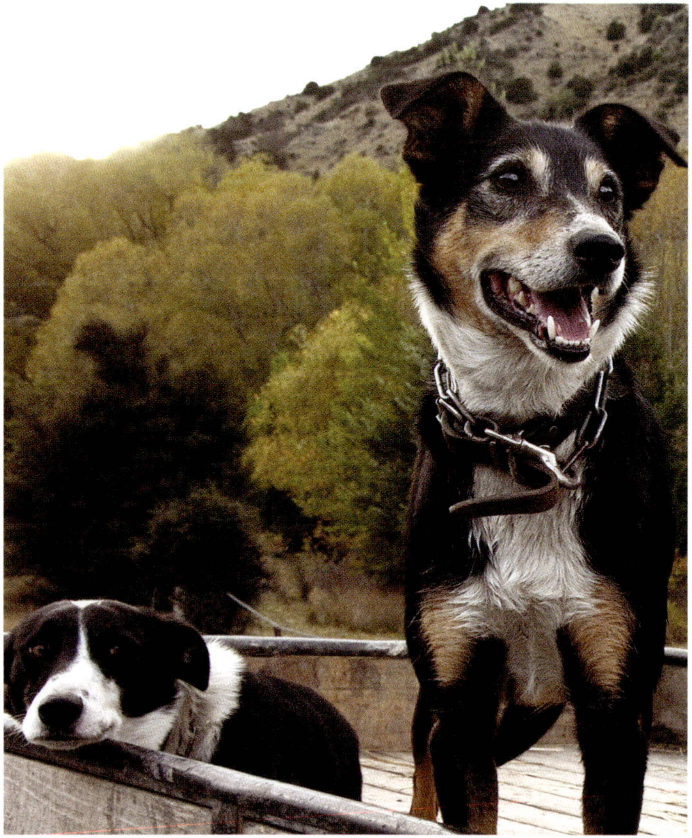

▲ Working dogs at Molesworth Station in Marlborough always look keen to go to work (well, most of them).

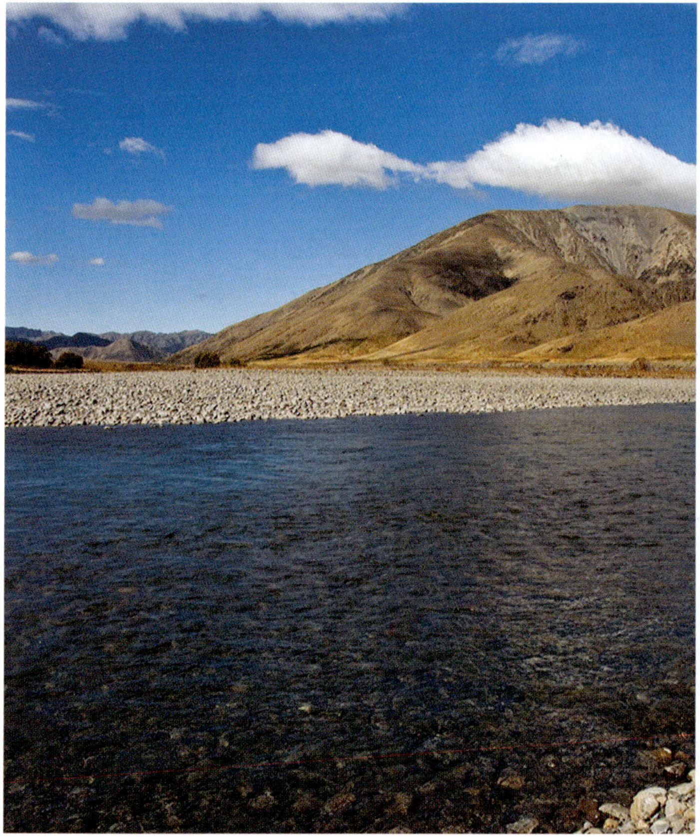

▲ The rivers and rugged landscape of this vast station have served as muse to many an artist.

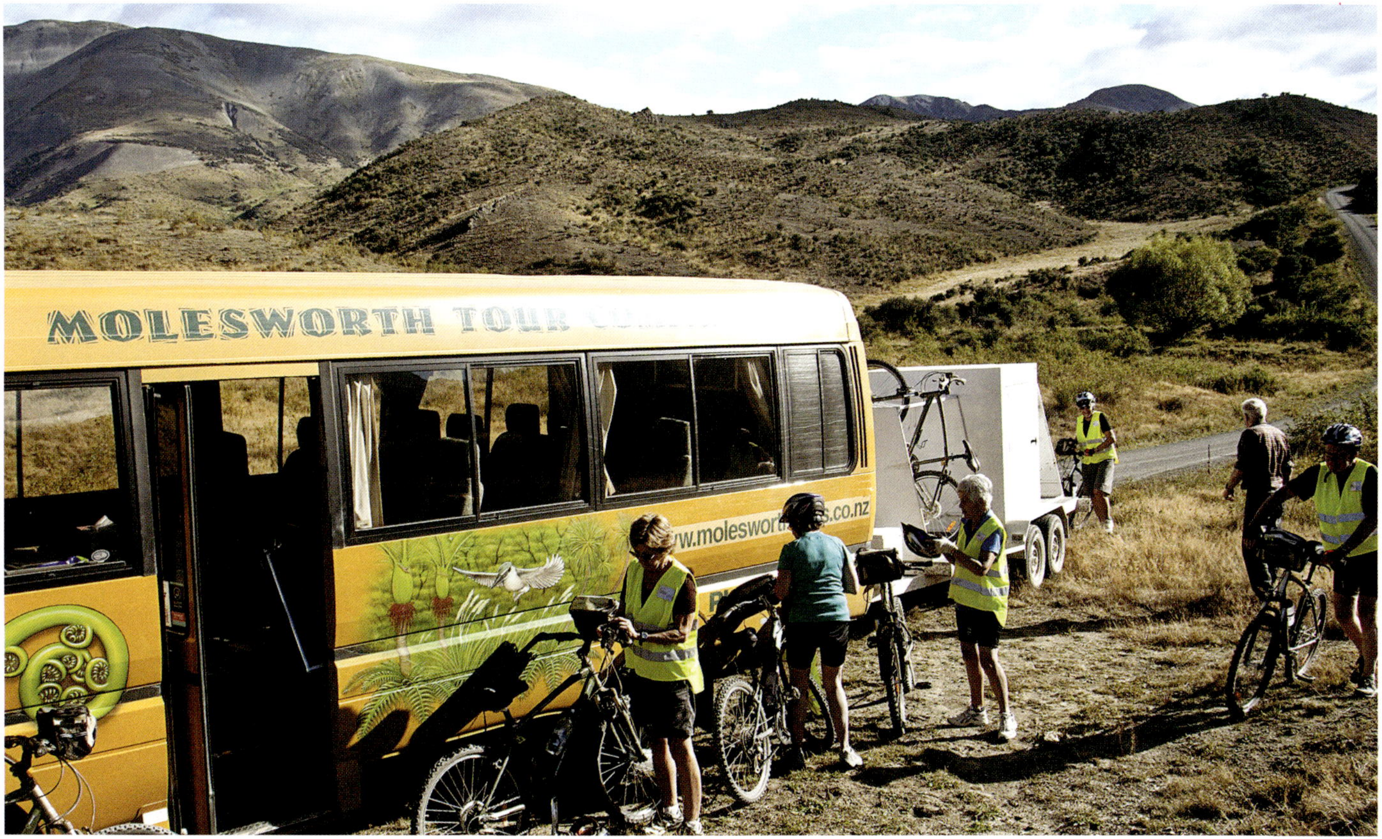

▲ A happy bunch of cross-country explorers take a well-earned rest.

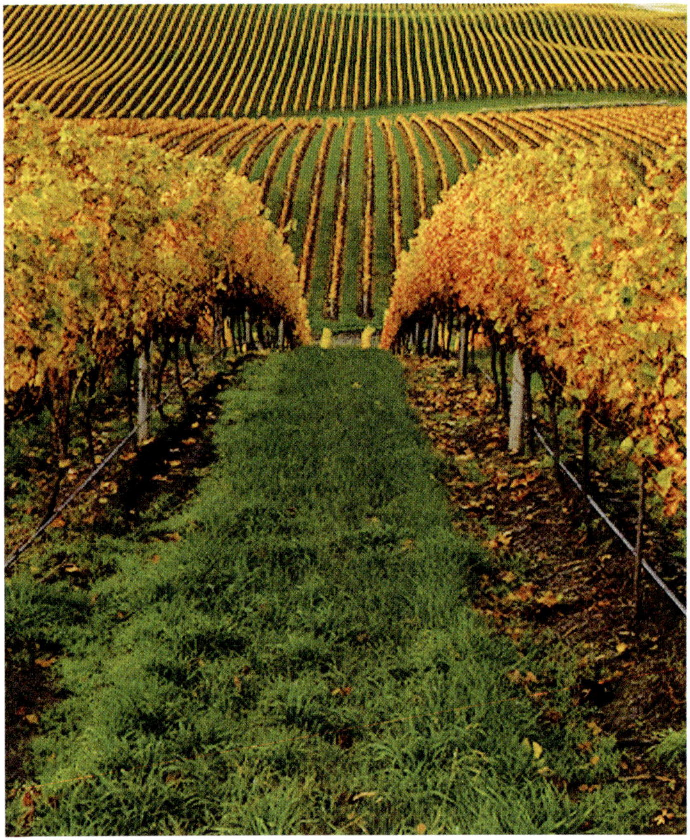

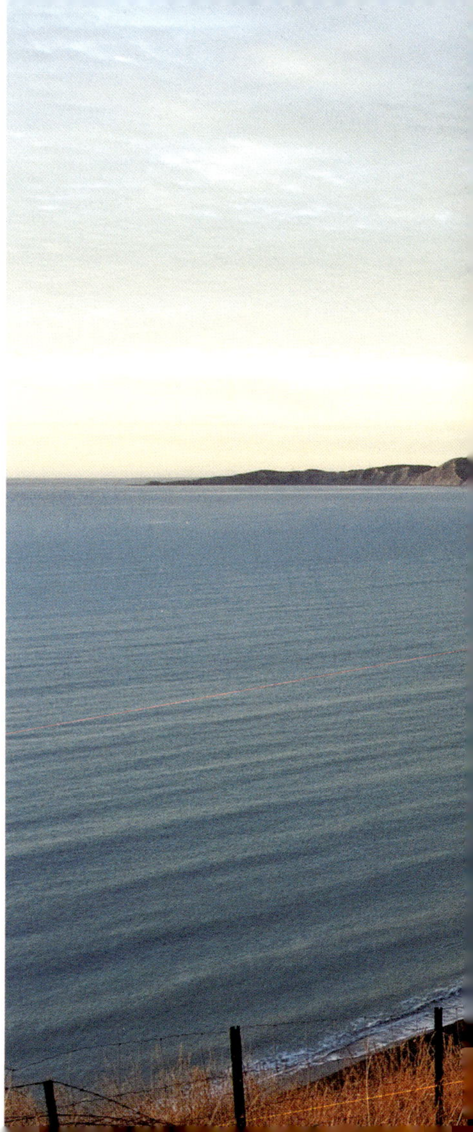

▲ Rows of vines turn burnt orange before my eyes at Yealands Estate Winery in Marlborough.

▶ Clifford Bay. First light breaks across Cook Strait, touches Cape Campbell and ignites the boundary fence on Yealands Estate.

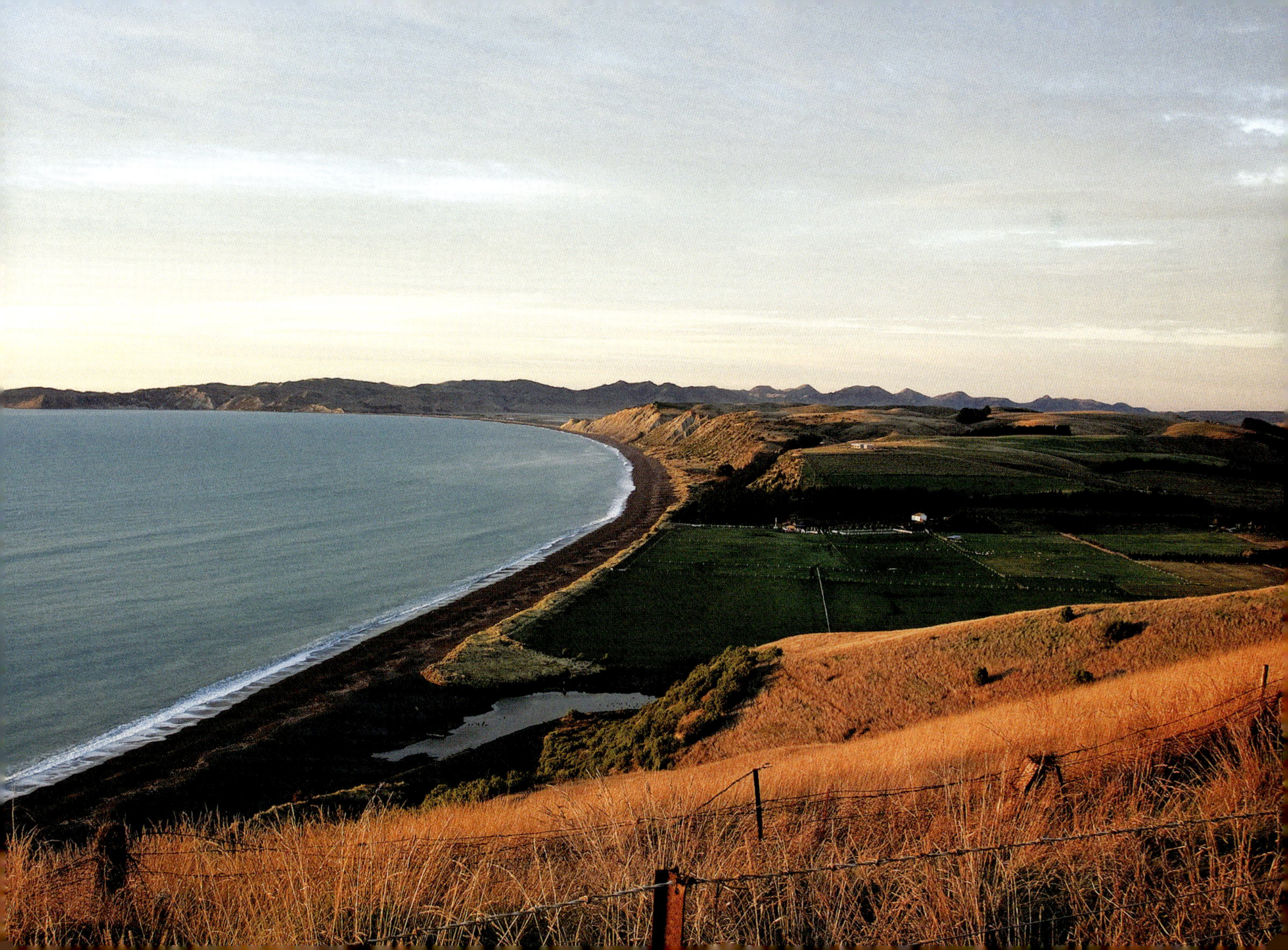

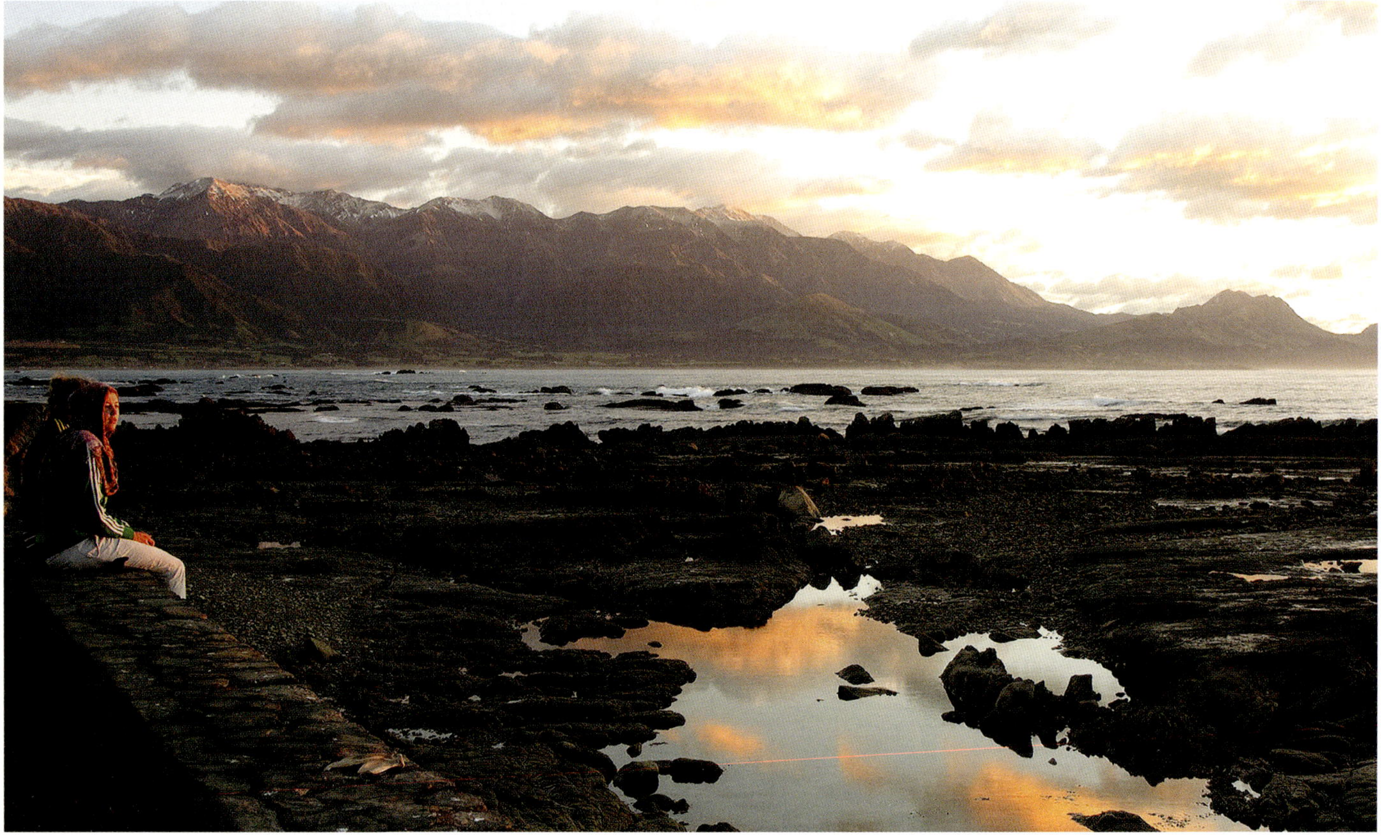

▲ You may need to reserve a space to see the sunrise here at the tip of the bay in Kaikoura.

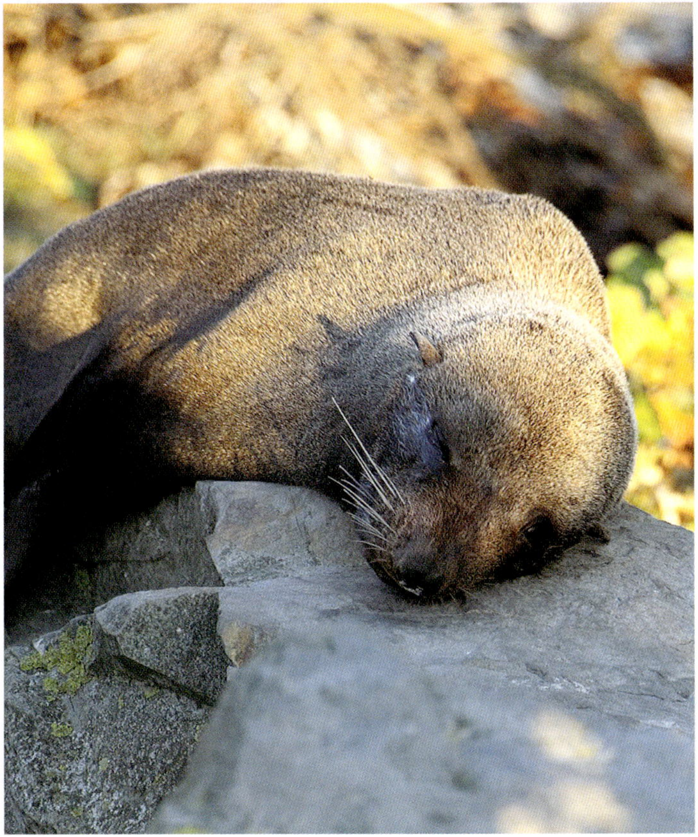

▲ An overnight guest in the carpark.

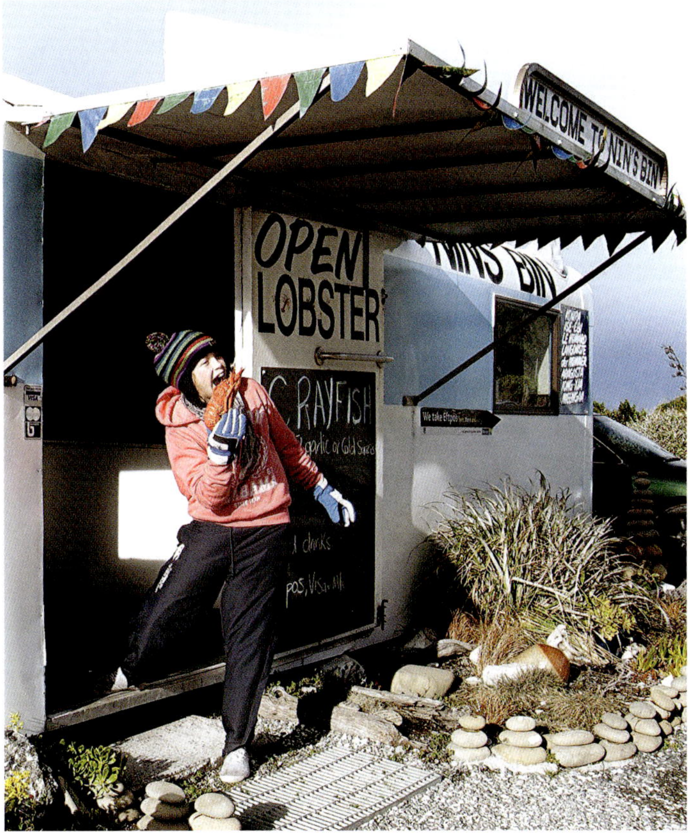

▲ Nin's Bin is an institution on the Kaikoura coast. It's always a relief to find it open and selling fresh crayfish.

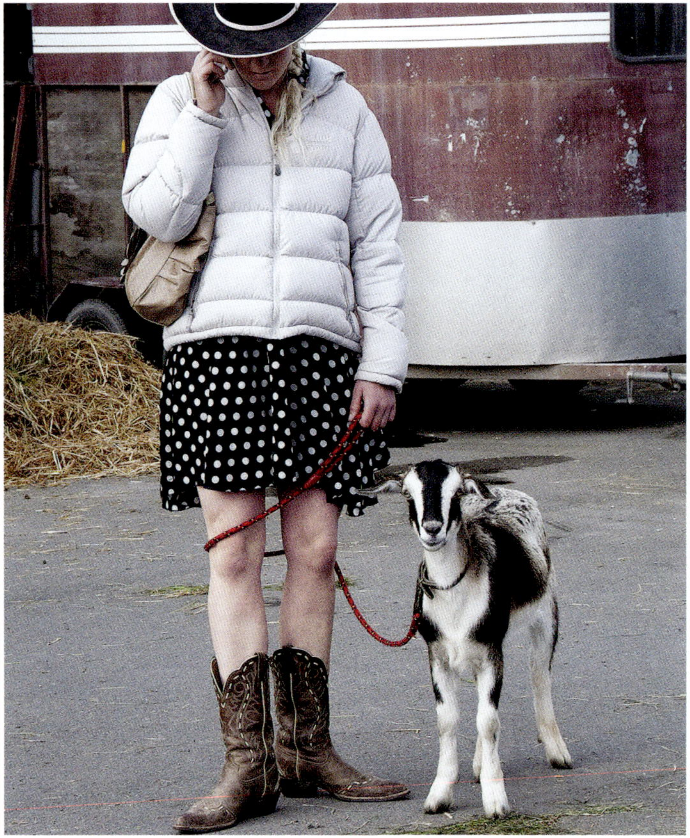

▲ It's a good idea to keep close to the boss at the 150th Canterbury A&P (Agricultural and Pastoral) Show near Christchurch.

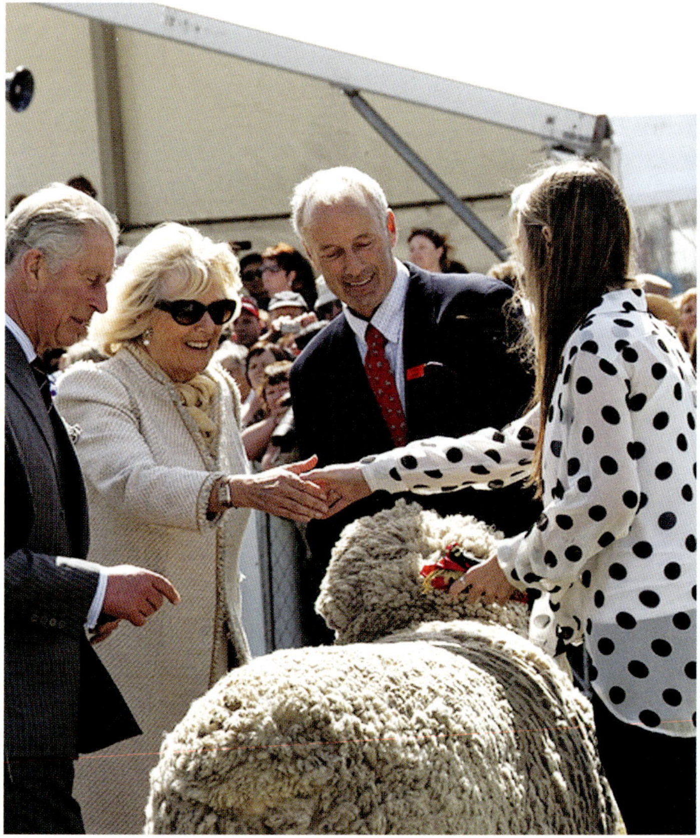

▲ It's not often one gets to rub shoulders with royalty. Here the Duke and Duchess of Cornwall greet a young exhibitor at the show with apparent delight.

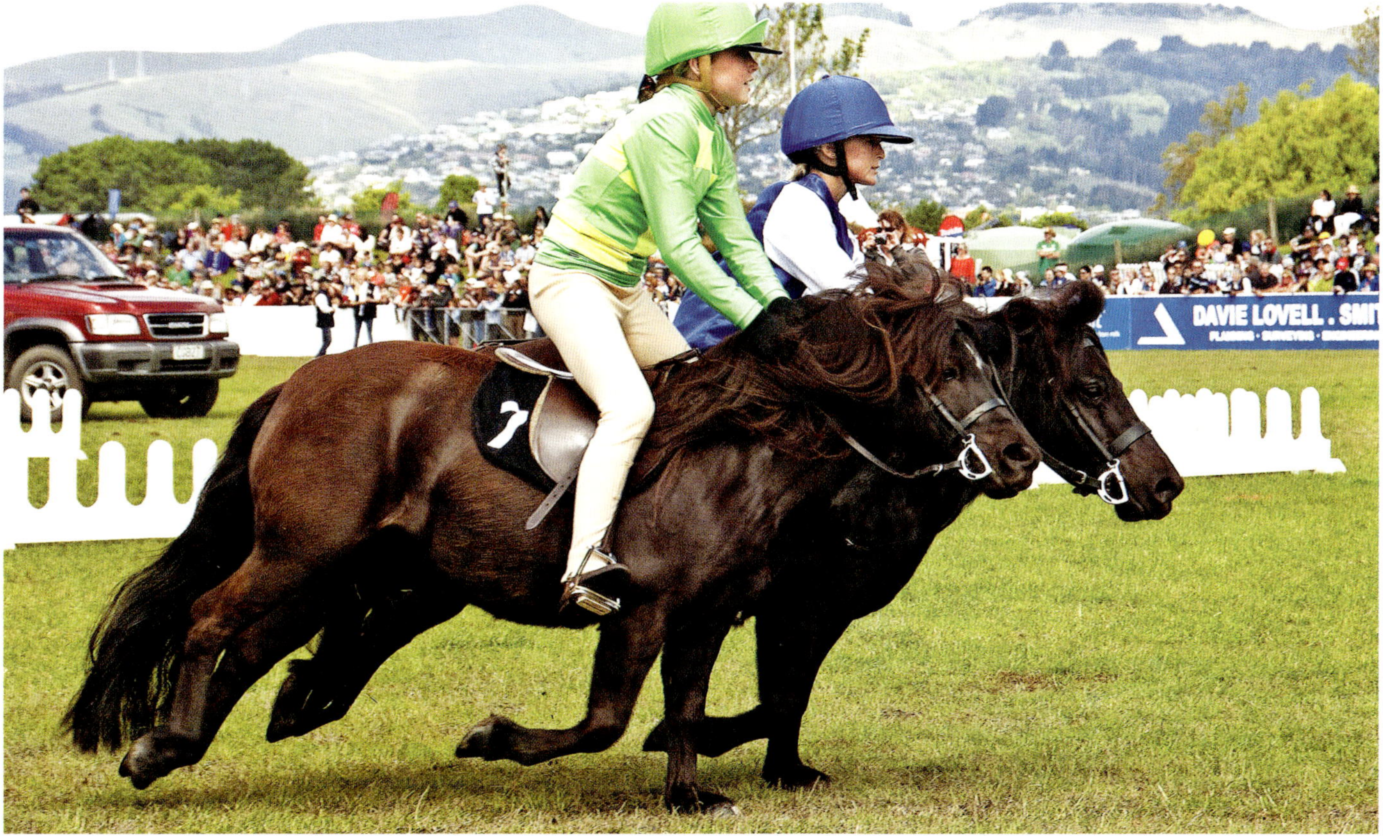

▲ Neck and neck as they race to the line, these ponies clearly know that royalty is watching.

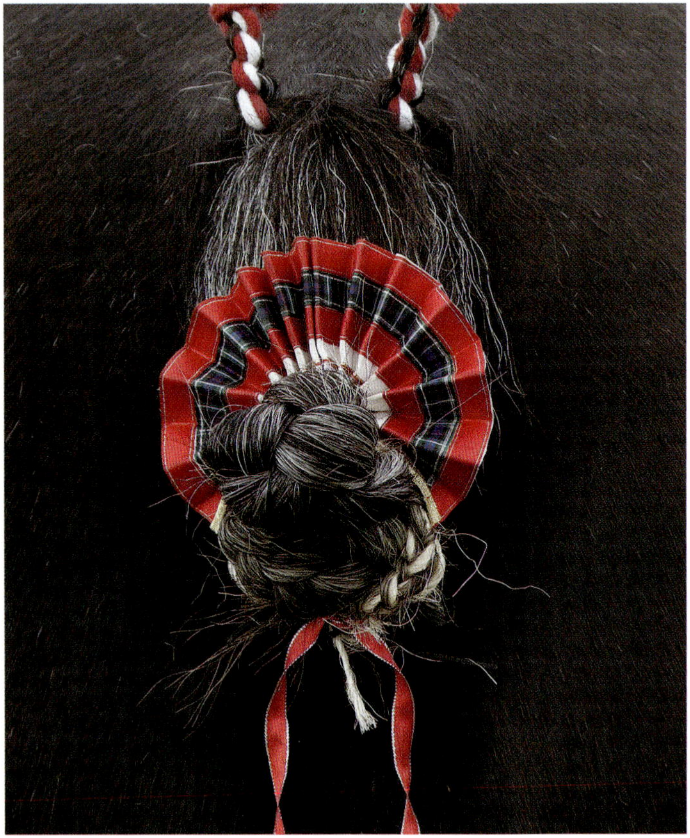

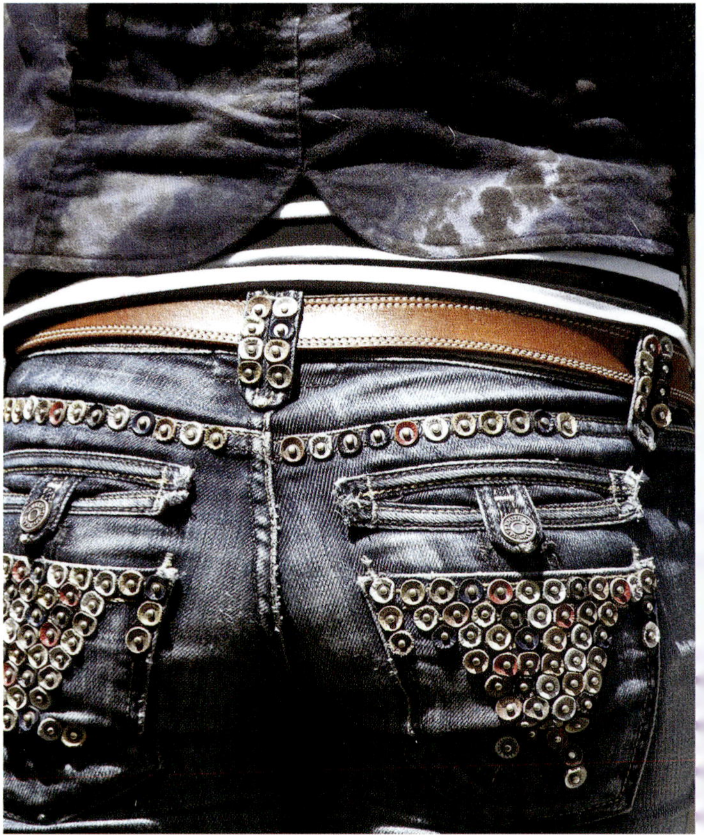

▲ Still at the A&P Show, a touch of glamour is accorded not just to the working Clydesdales but also their handlers.

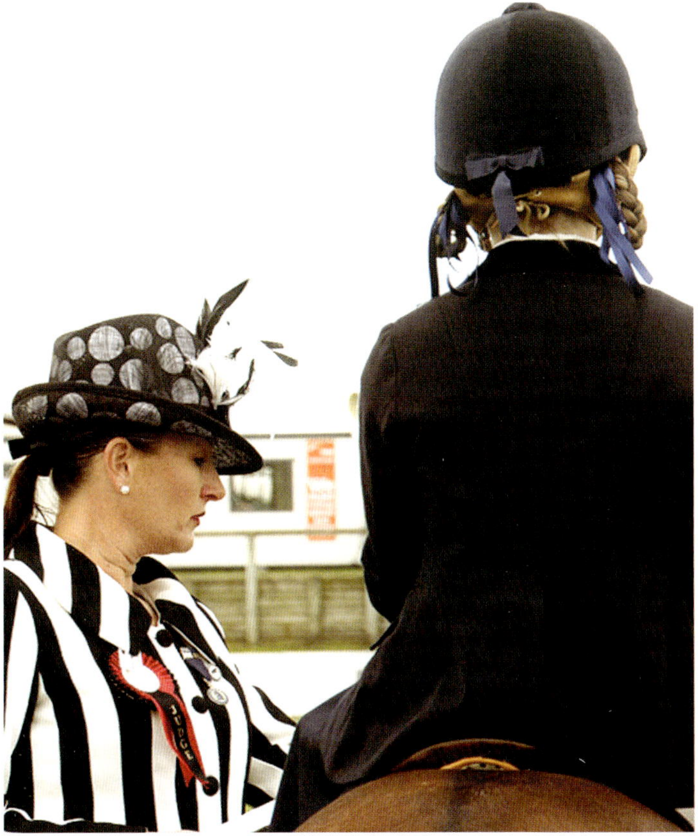

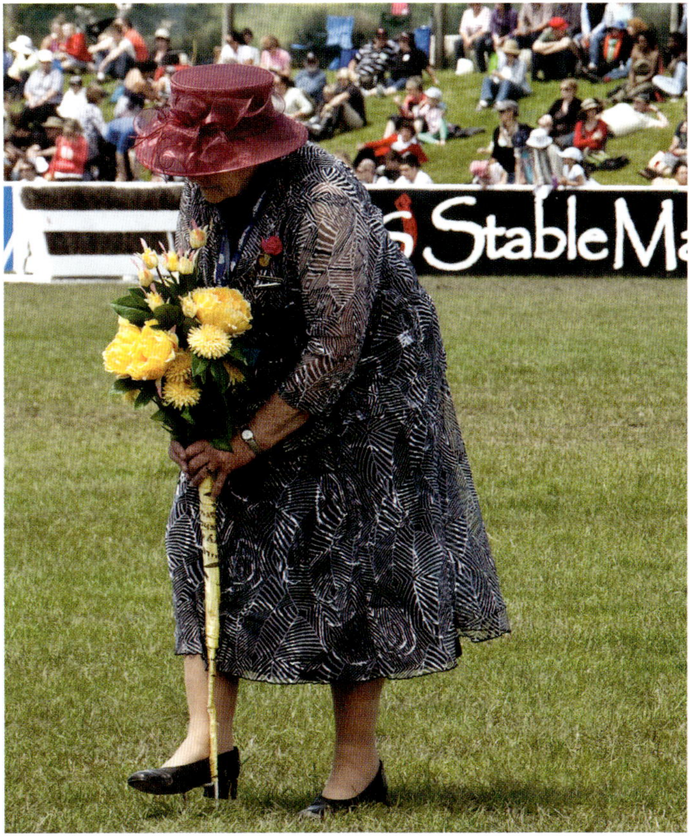

▲ Stylish headgear is everywhere – in the stable and in the show ring.

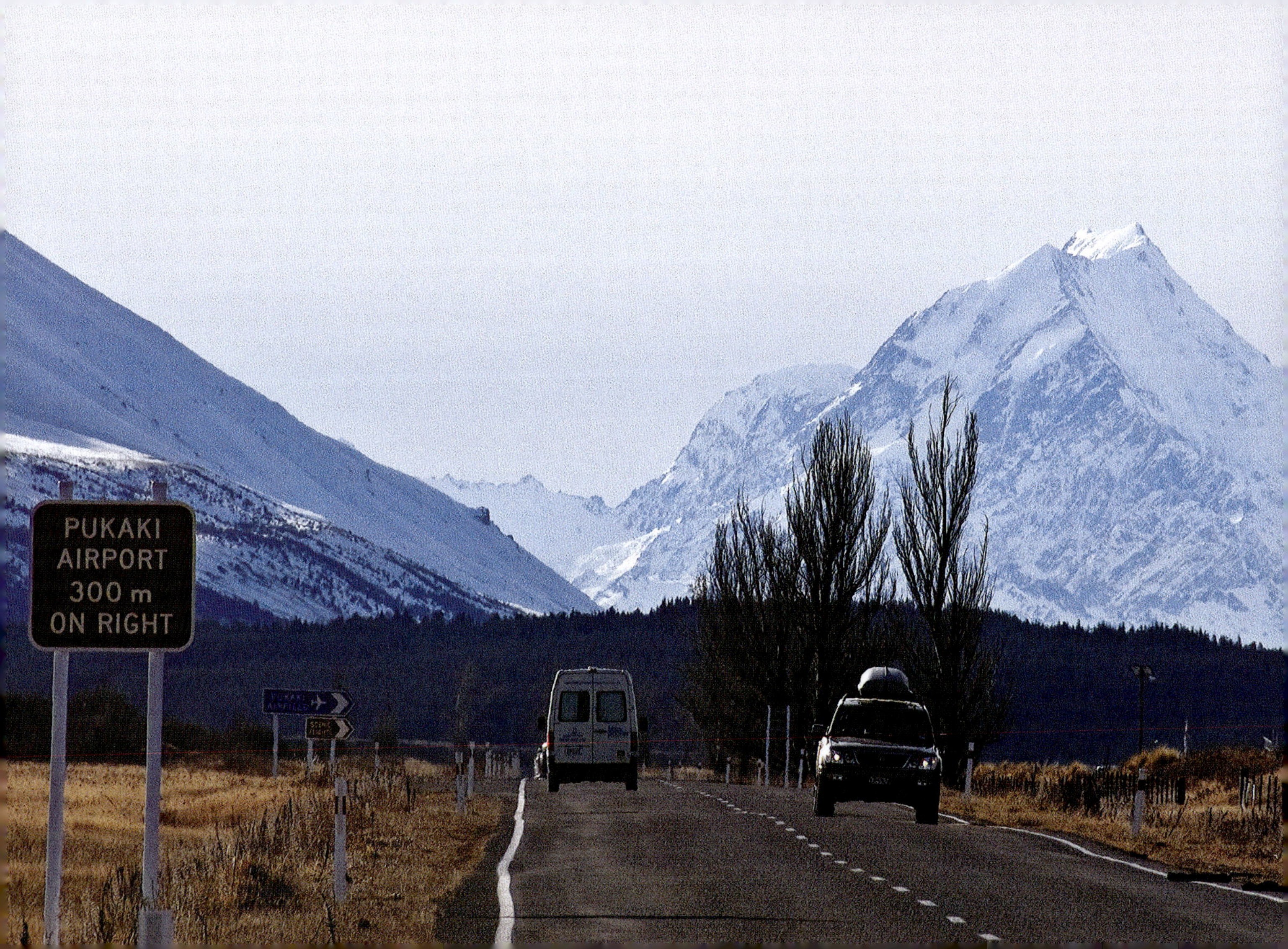
PUKAKI
AIRPORT
300 m
ON RIGHT

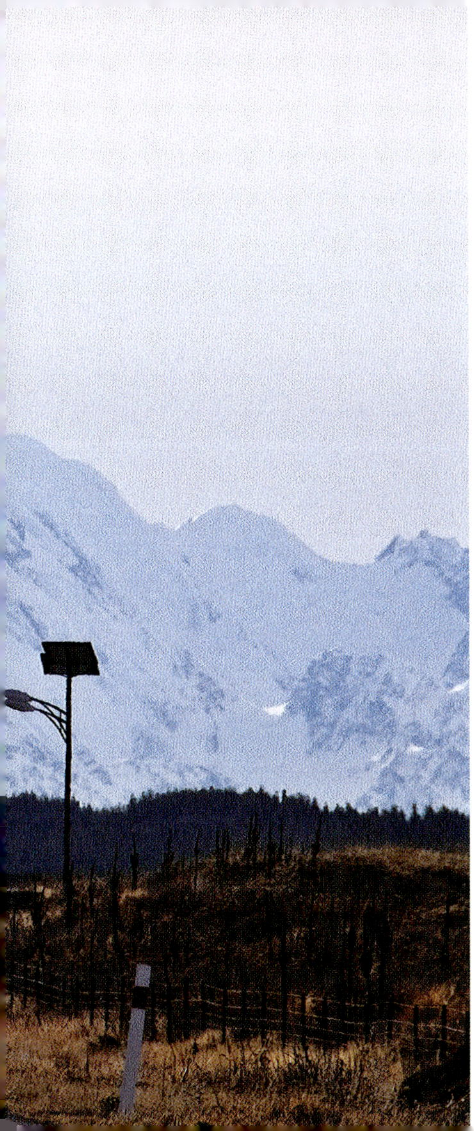

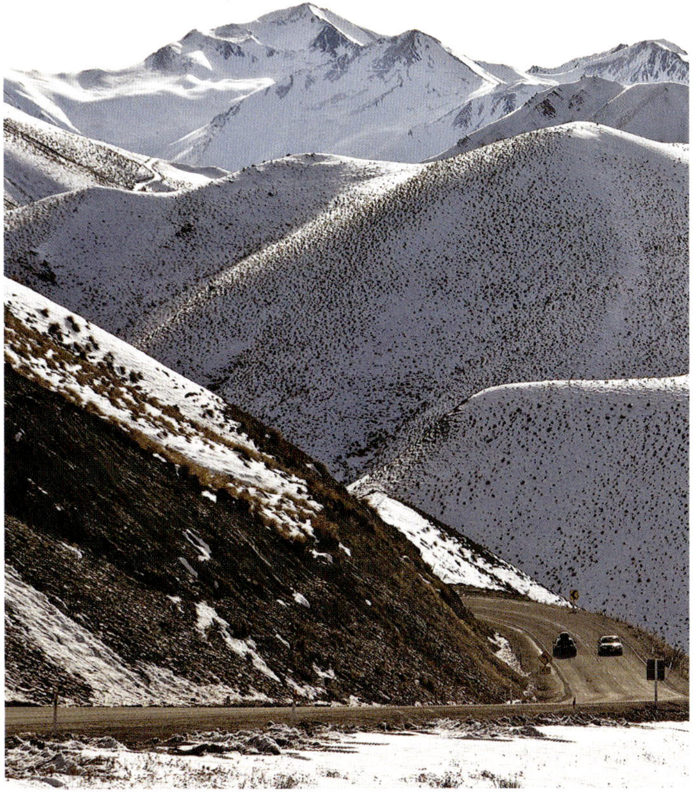

▲ Lindis Pass, Otago. I'm always challenged by this landscape and find myself stopping around every corner to take a closer look.

◀ Aoraki Mount Cook, framed and clearly visible from the road.

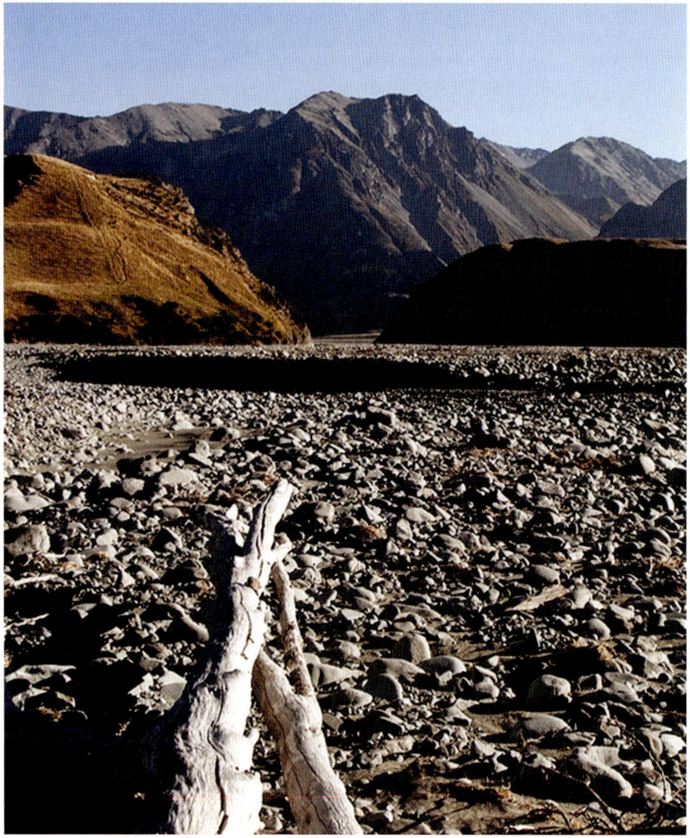

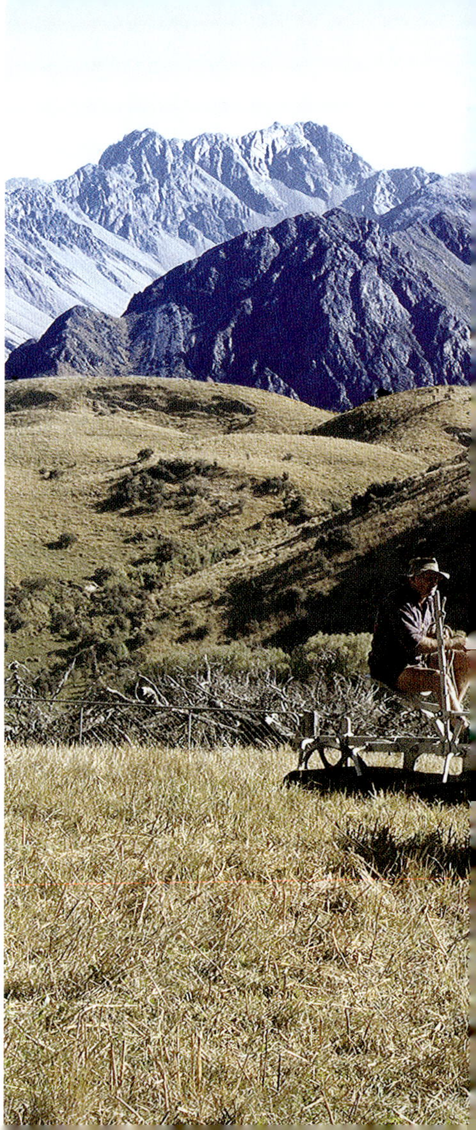

▲ The headwaters of the Rakaia River seen here in summer. In spring, this spot is flooded from bank to bank with the rush of snow melt.

▶ Erewhon Station (Nowhere spelled backwards), Canterbury. You can tell that these gentle giants love their work.

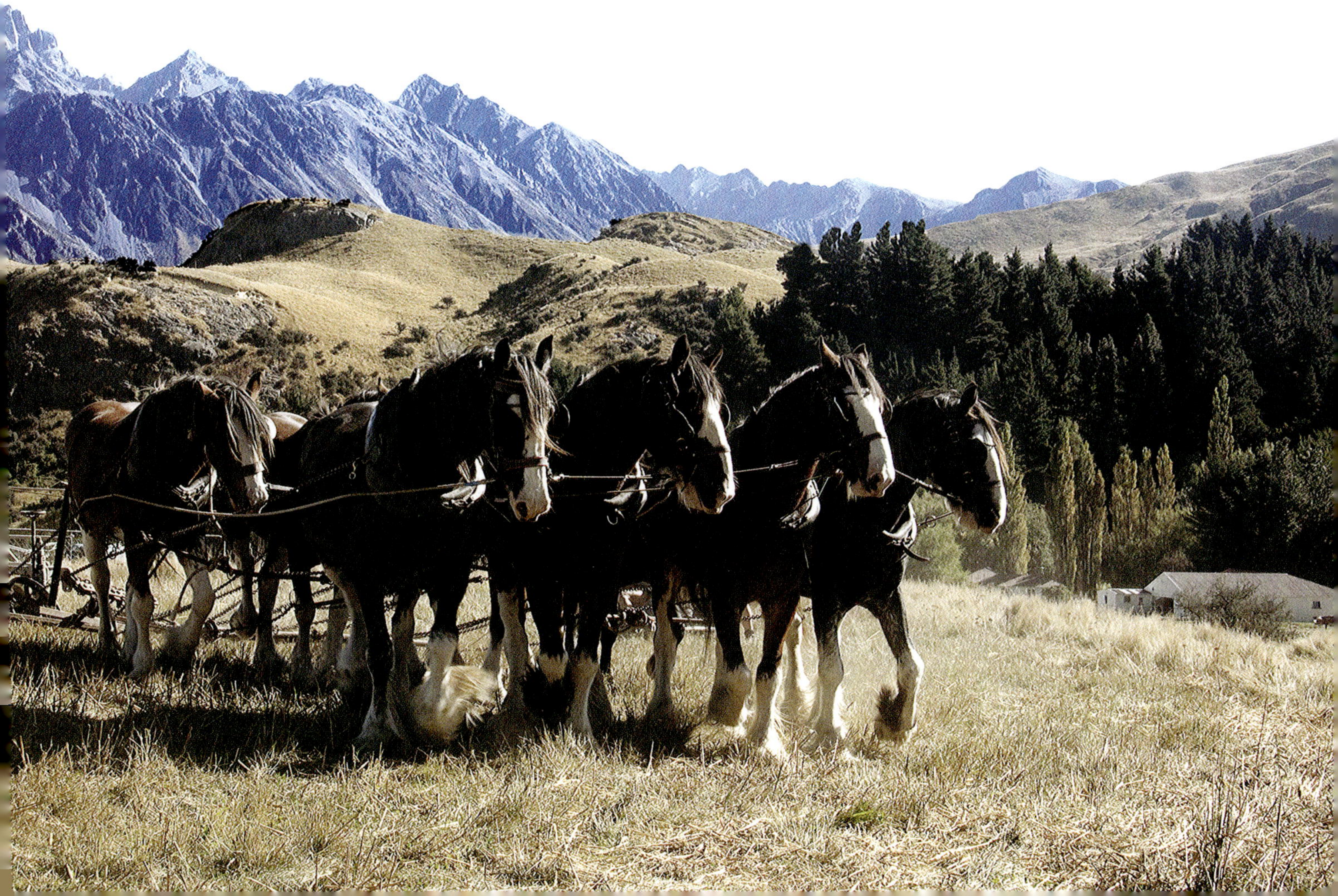

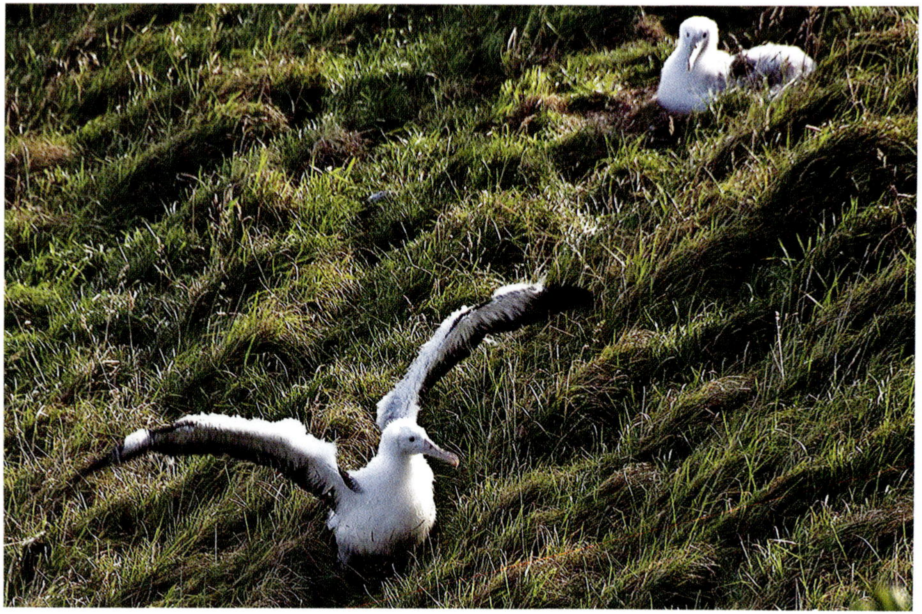

▲ Testing the wind on the slopes of the Otago Peninsula, the young albatross chick will soon take flight.

▶ The cargo on this ship seems almost close enough to touch as it slips through the narrow channel into Port Otago.

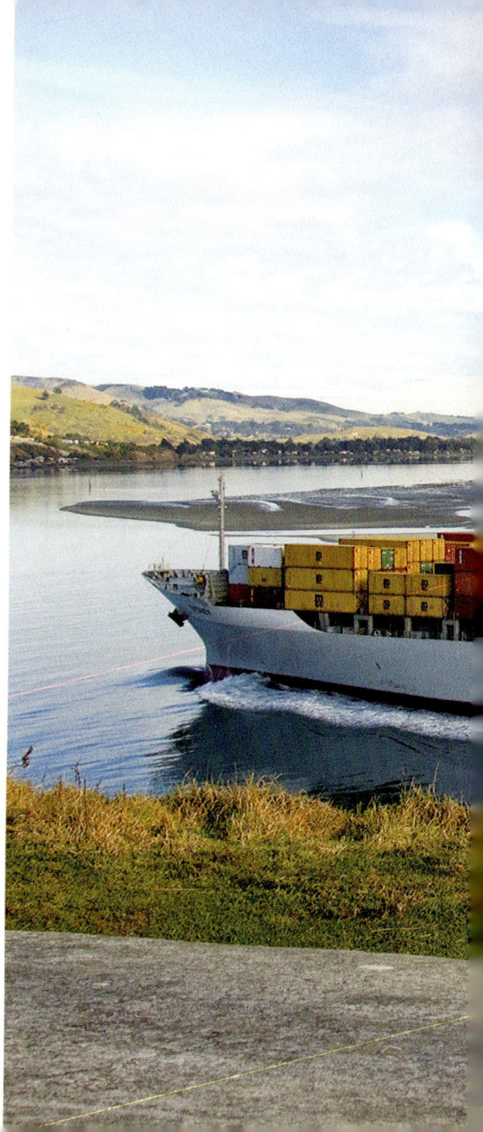

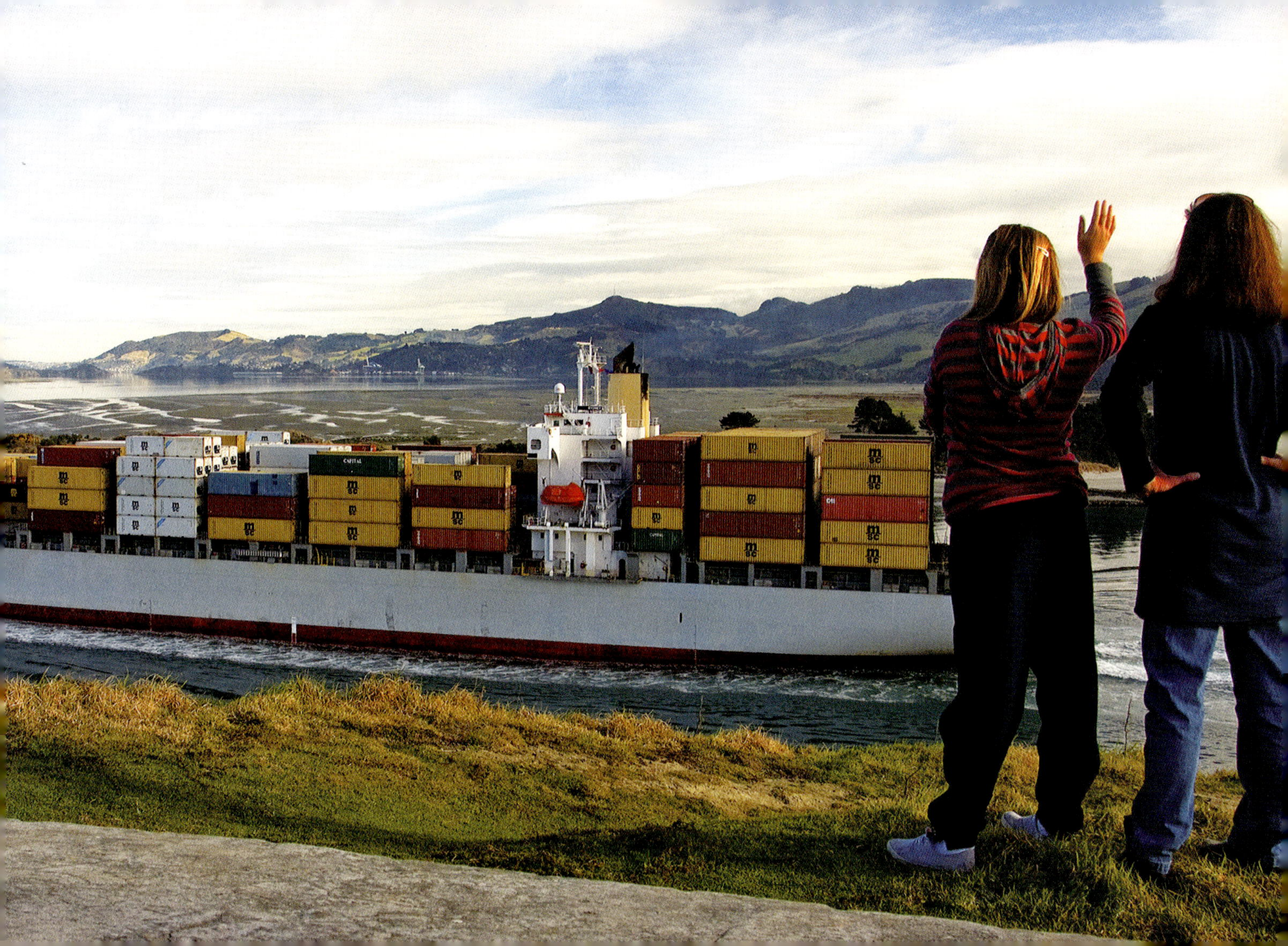

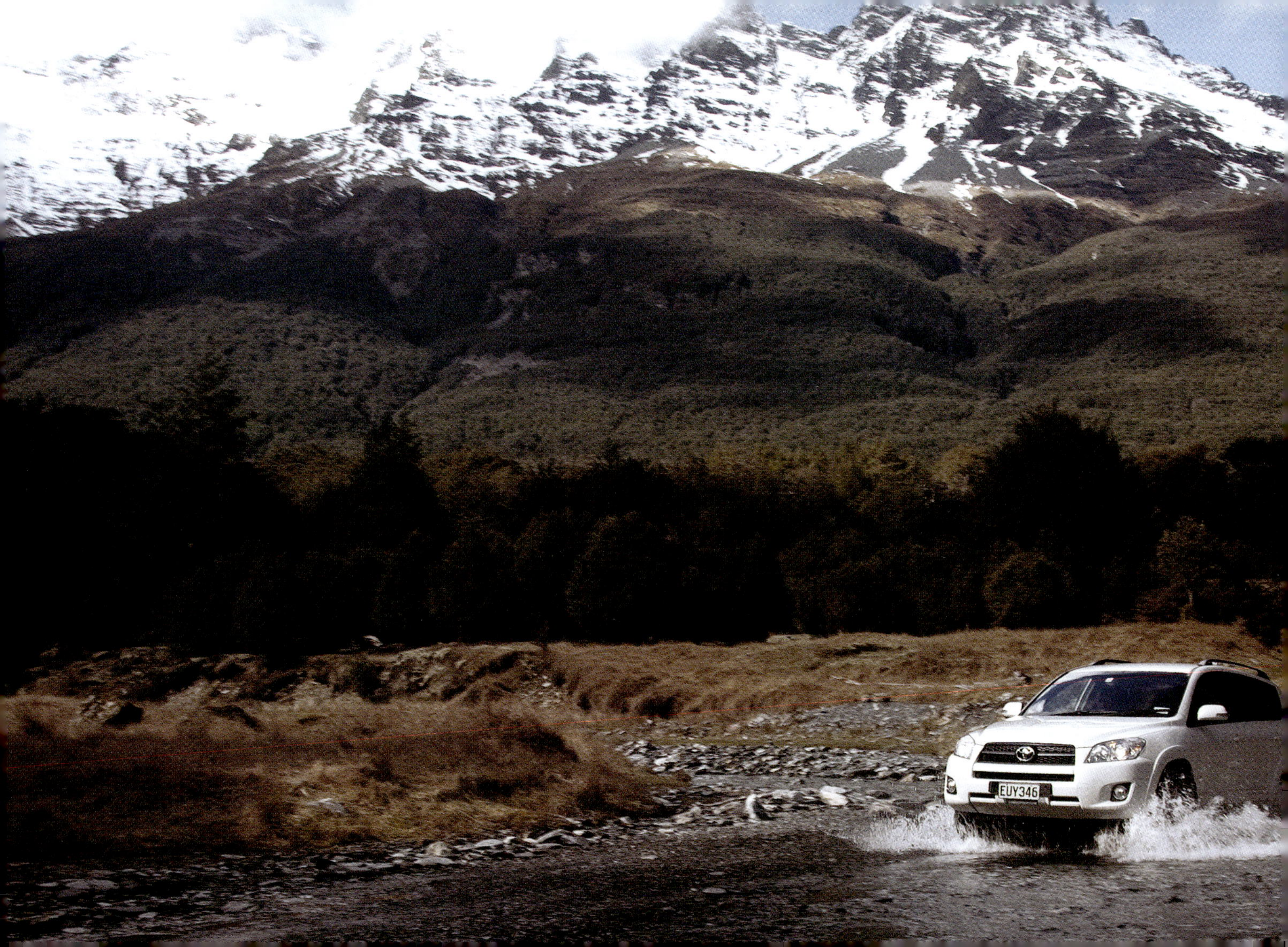
EUY346

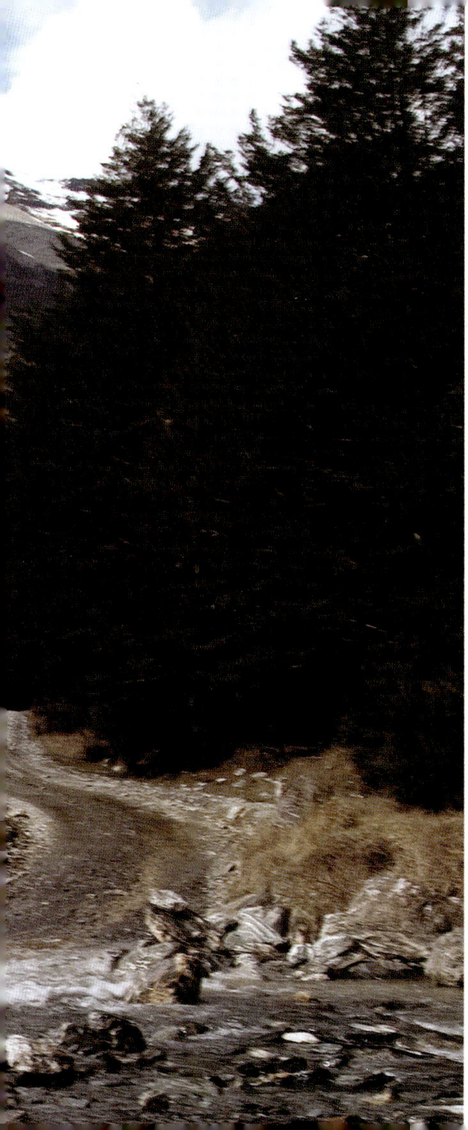

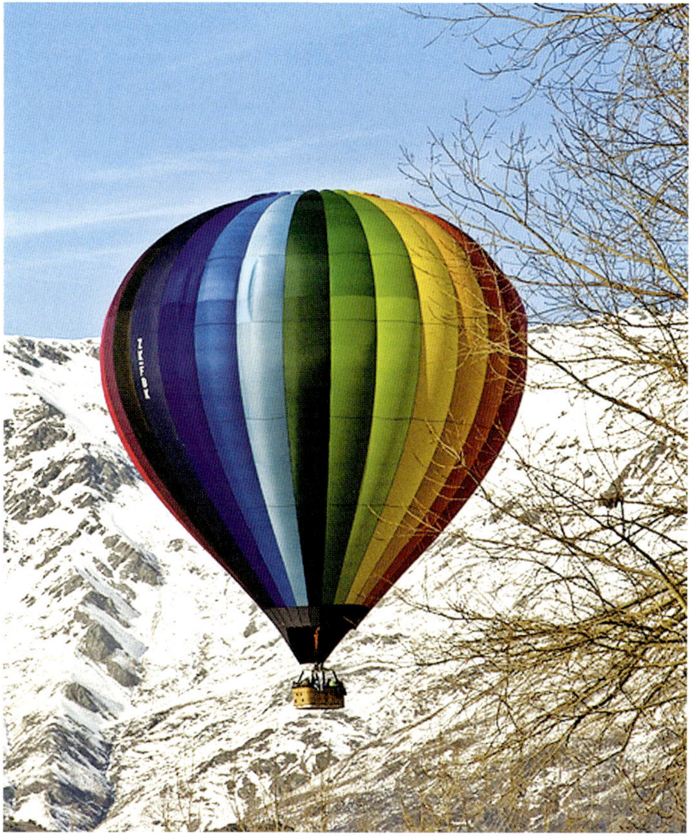

▲ Queenstown, Central Otago. En route to Arrowtown, vibrantly coloured hot air balloons loom large against new snow.

◀ There's nothing like an exhilarating dash in a 4x4 through the snow-fed streams of Central Otago's Dart Valley.

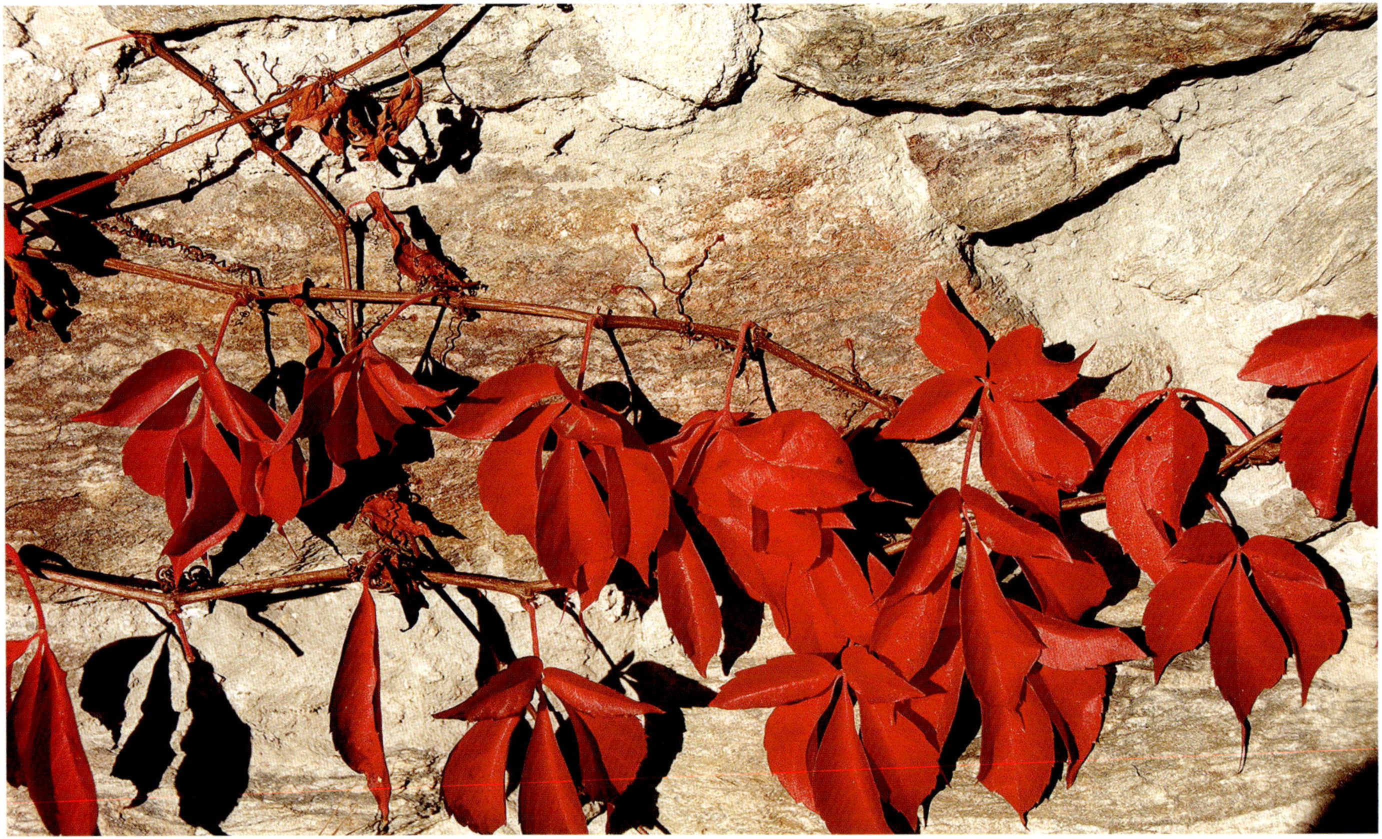

▲ Cromwell, Central Otago. A drystone wall makes the perfect background for these richly hued vines in one of New Zealand's best known wine-growing regions.

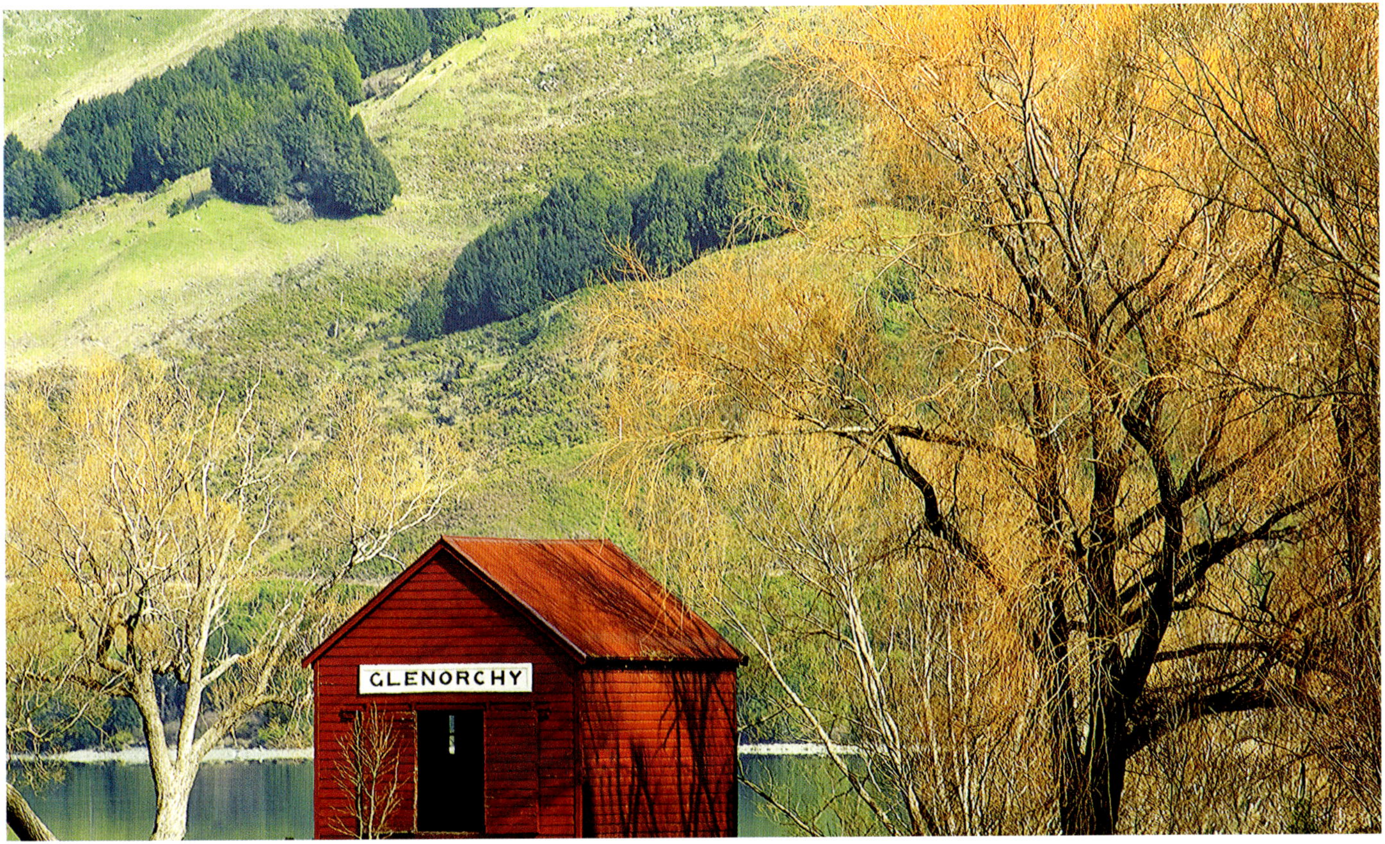

▲ Glenorchy on the shores of Lake Wakatipu, where the adventures range from jet boat rides to walking tracks, and a lot of fly fishing in between.

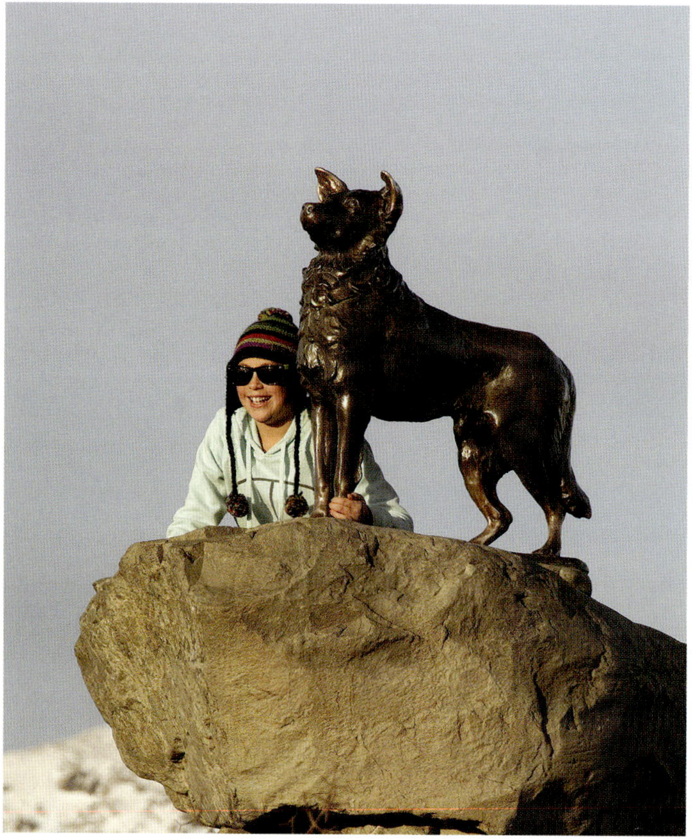

▲ McKenzie's dog at Lake Tekapo. Standing sentinel on this rock, he's never alone for long.

▶ Dawn lends a lavender hue to an idyllic spot, beside Lake Tekapo.

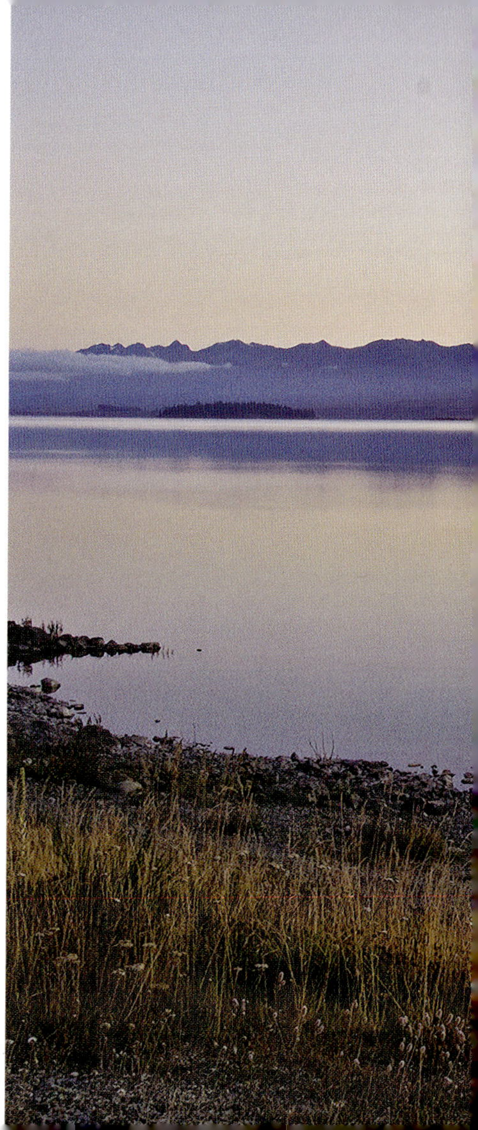

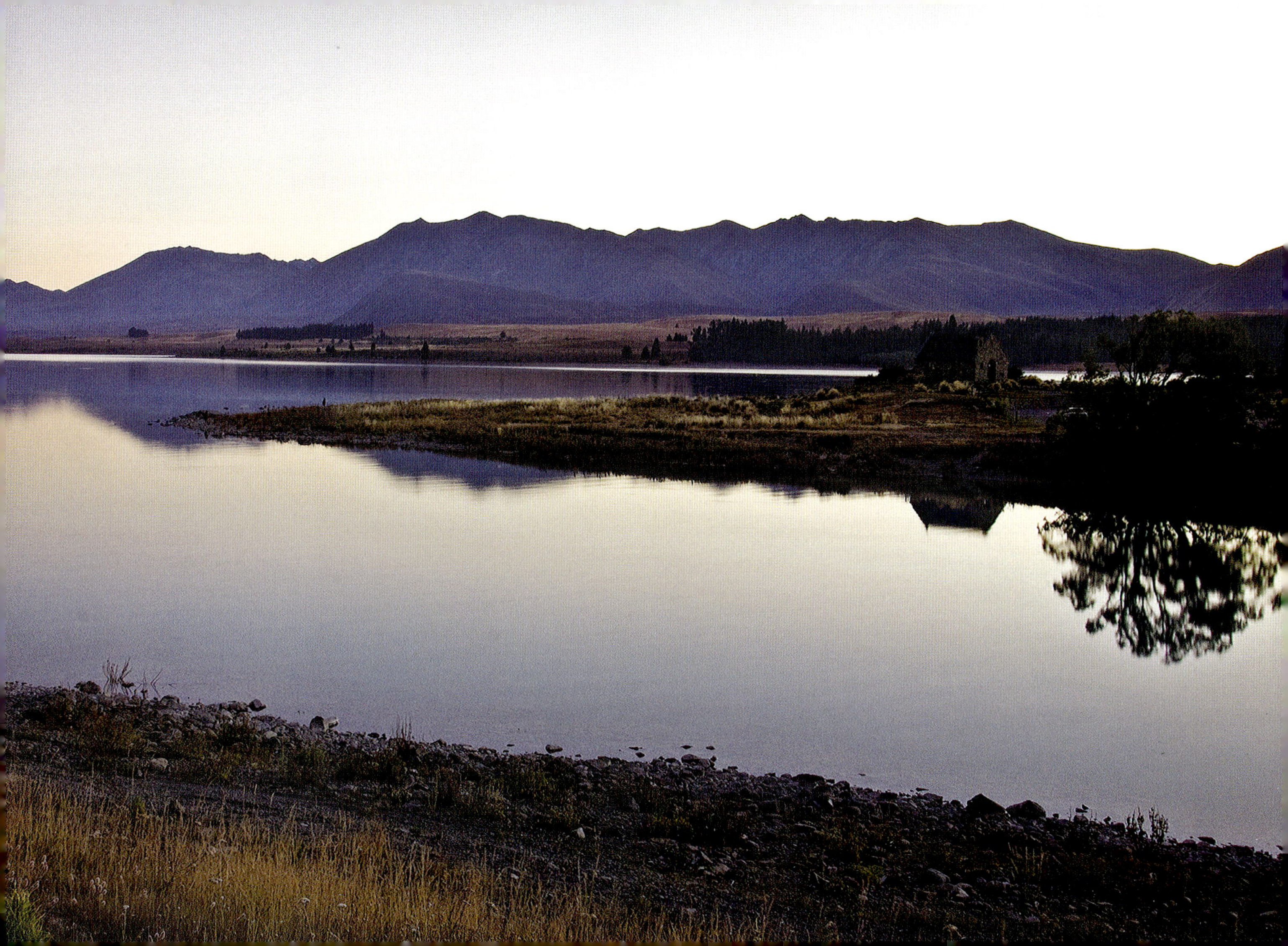

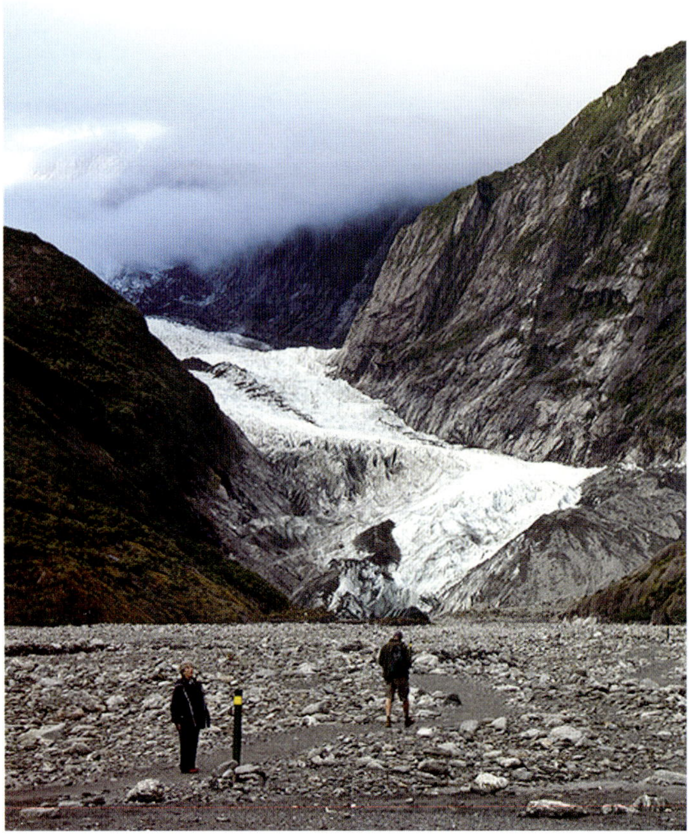

▲ The Franz Josef Glacier leaves me feeling very small in comparison.

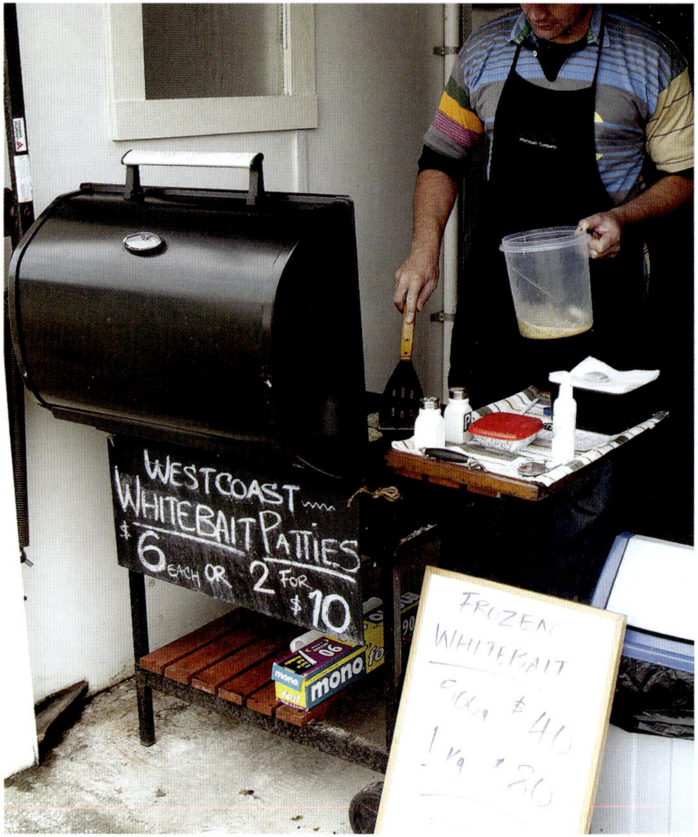

▲ Over in Hokitika, be sure to enjoy some fresh West Coast whitebait fritters straight from a hot plate and wrapped in soft brown bread. Don't forget the lemon – and wipe off that butter dribbling down your chin.

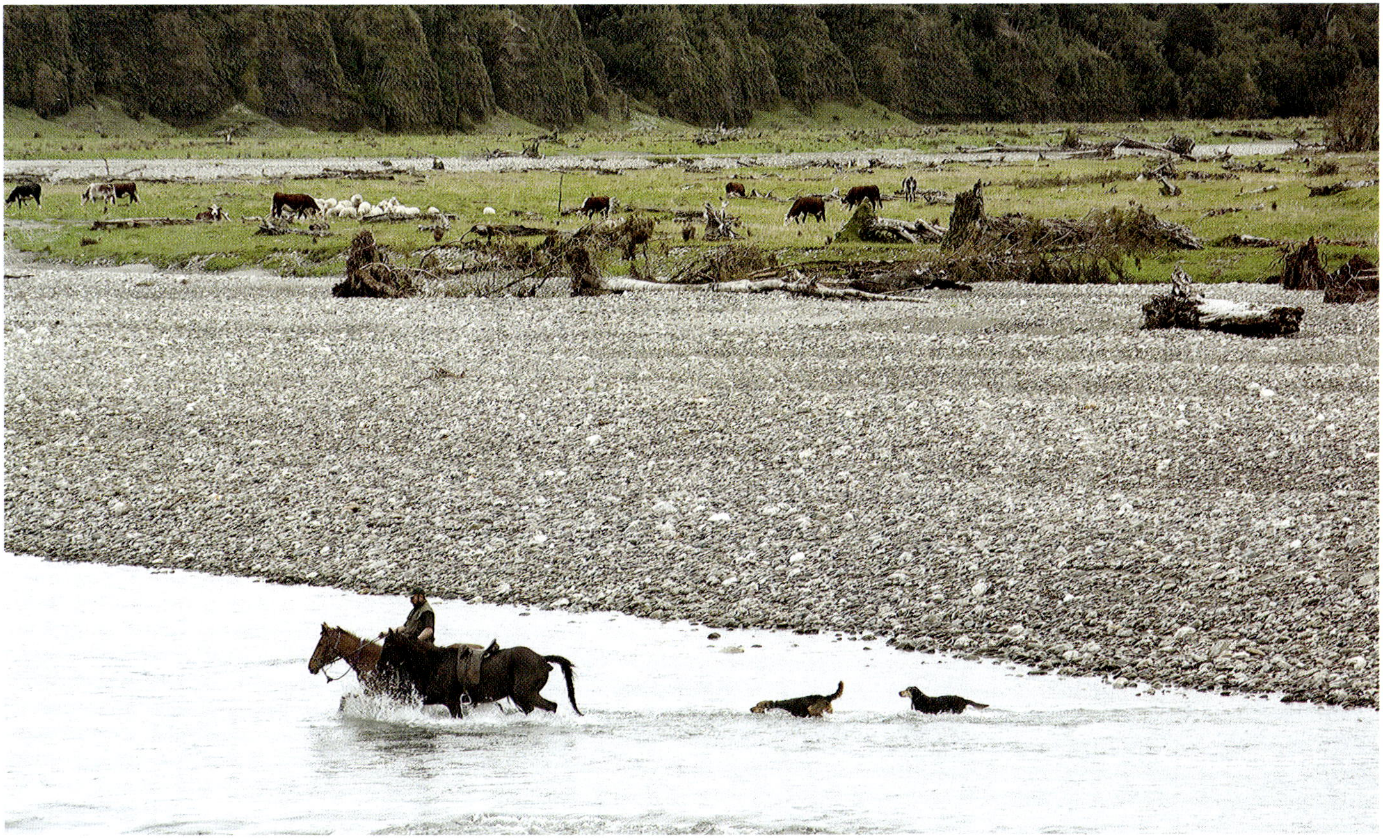

▲ A man, his horse, and two faithful workers – a small window into rural life on the West Coast as we pass by.

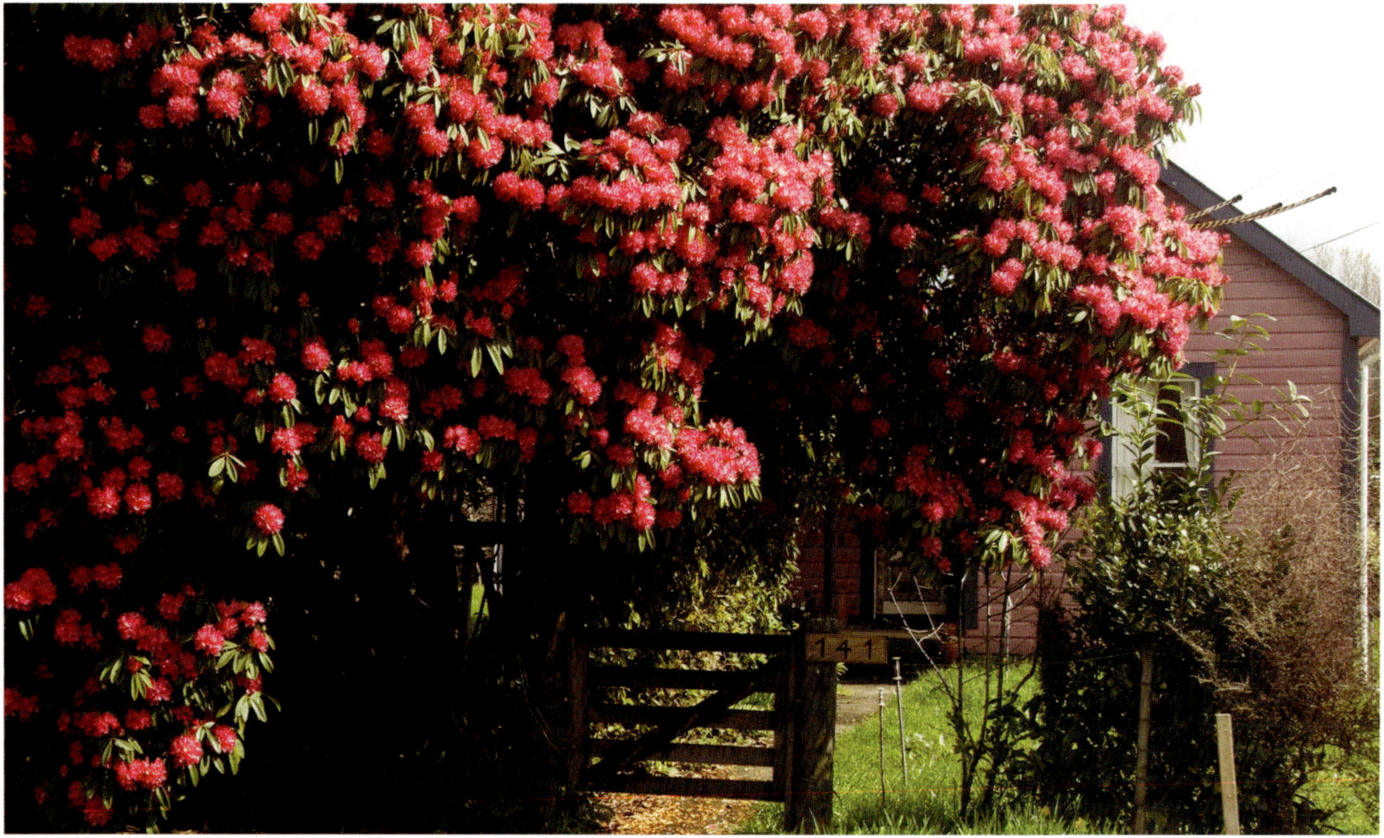

▲ Blackball, a small town on the West Coast, is the birthplace of New Zealand's Labour Party. This aged – and aptly red – rhododendron must have some stories to tell.

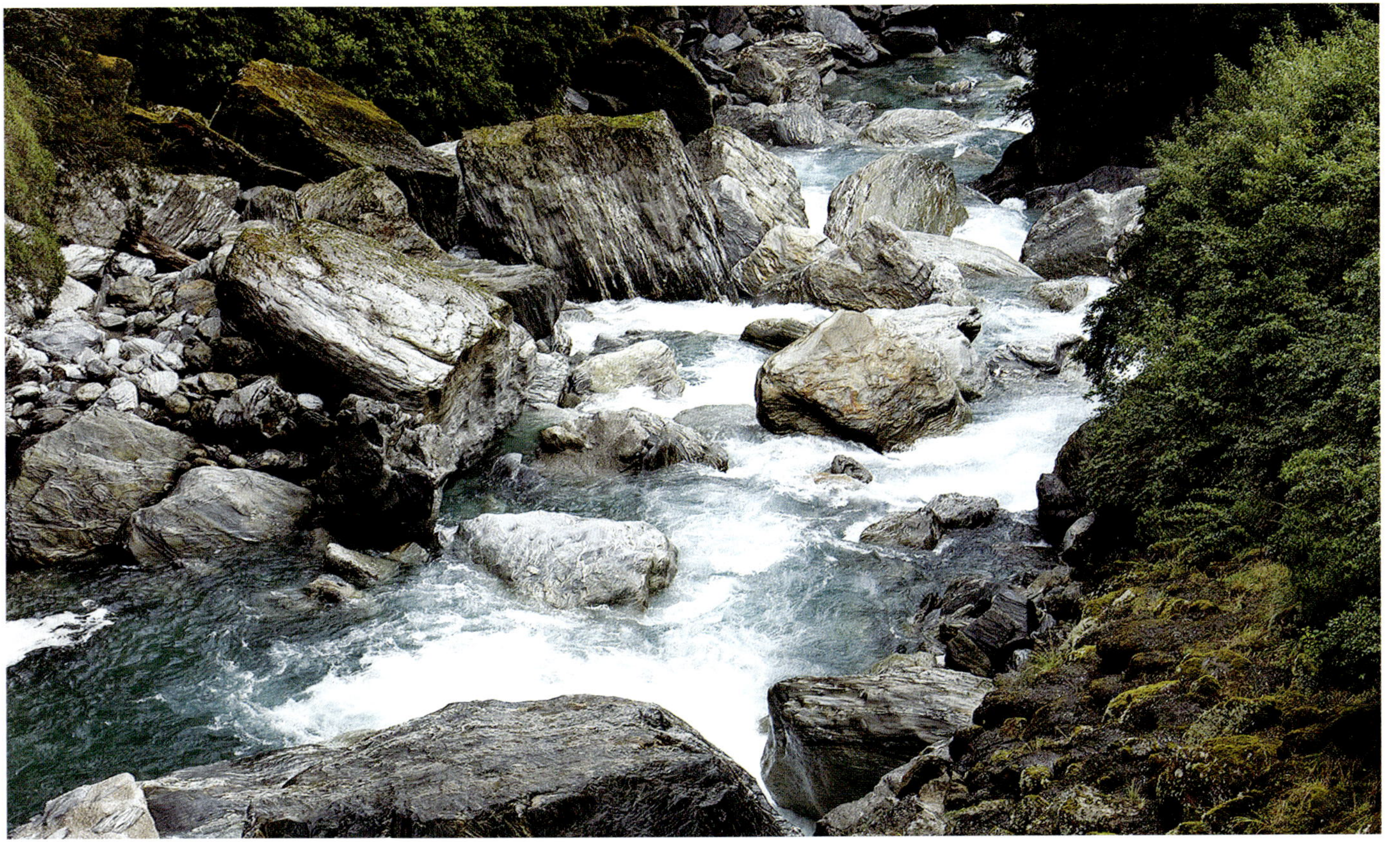

▲ The makings of an artwork are laid out in the glacial waters of the Haast River.

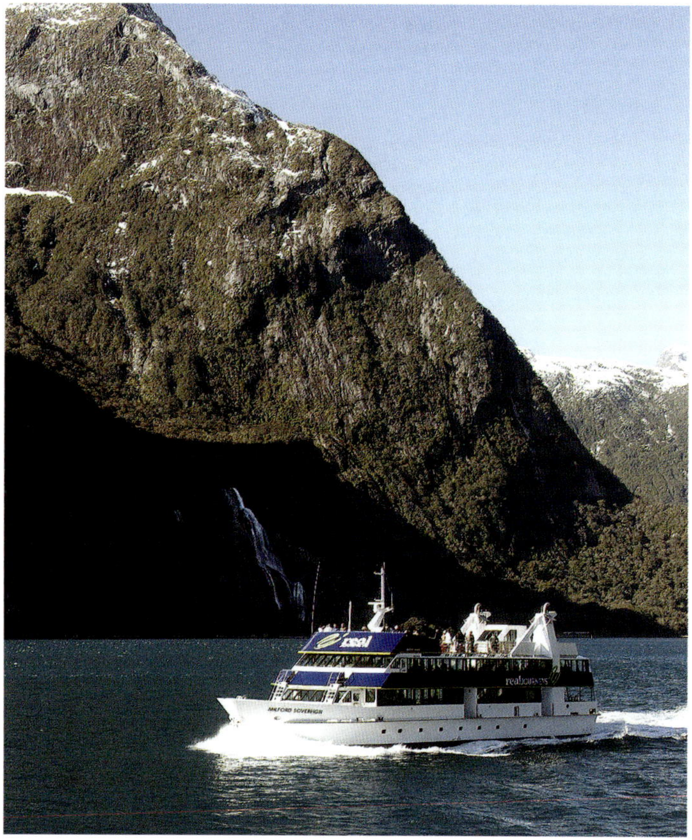

▲ Just getting down to Milford Sound is exciting enough, then there's the trip on the water, which is breathtaking.

▶ I feel an emotional connection with the dolphins: they seem to know when you're watching them play.

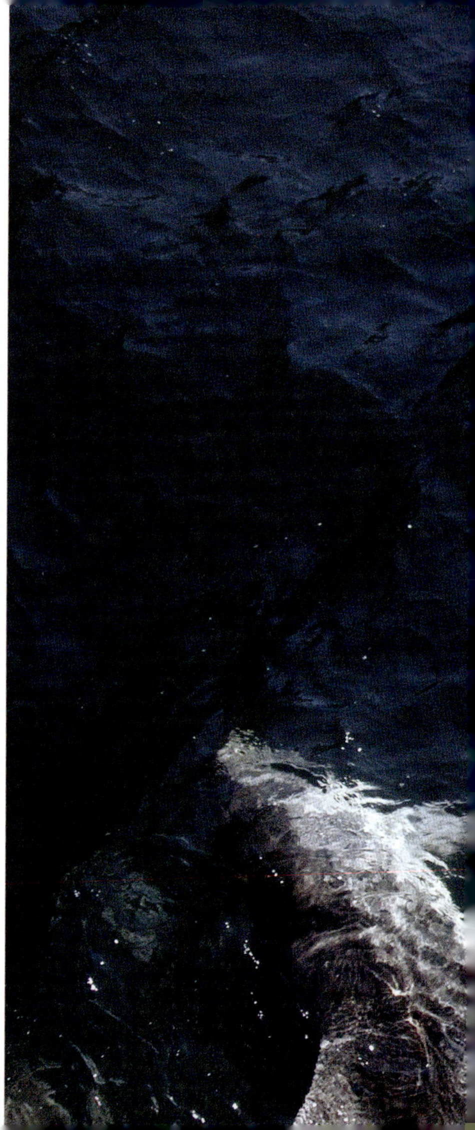

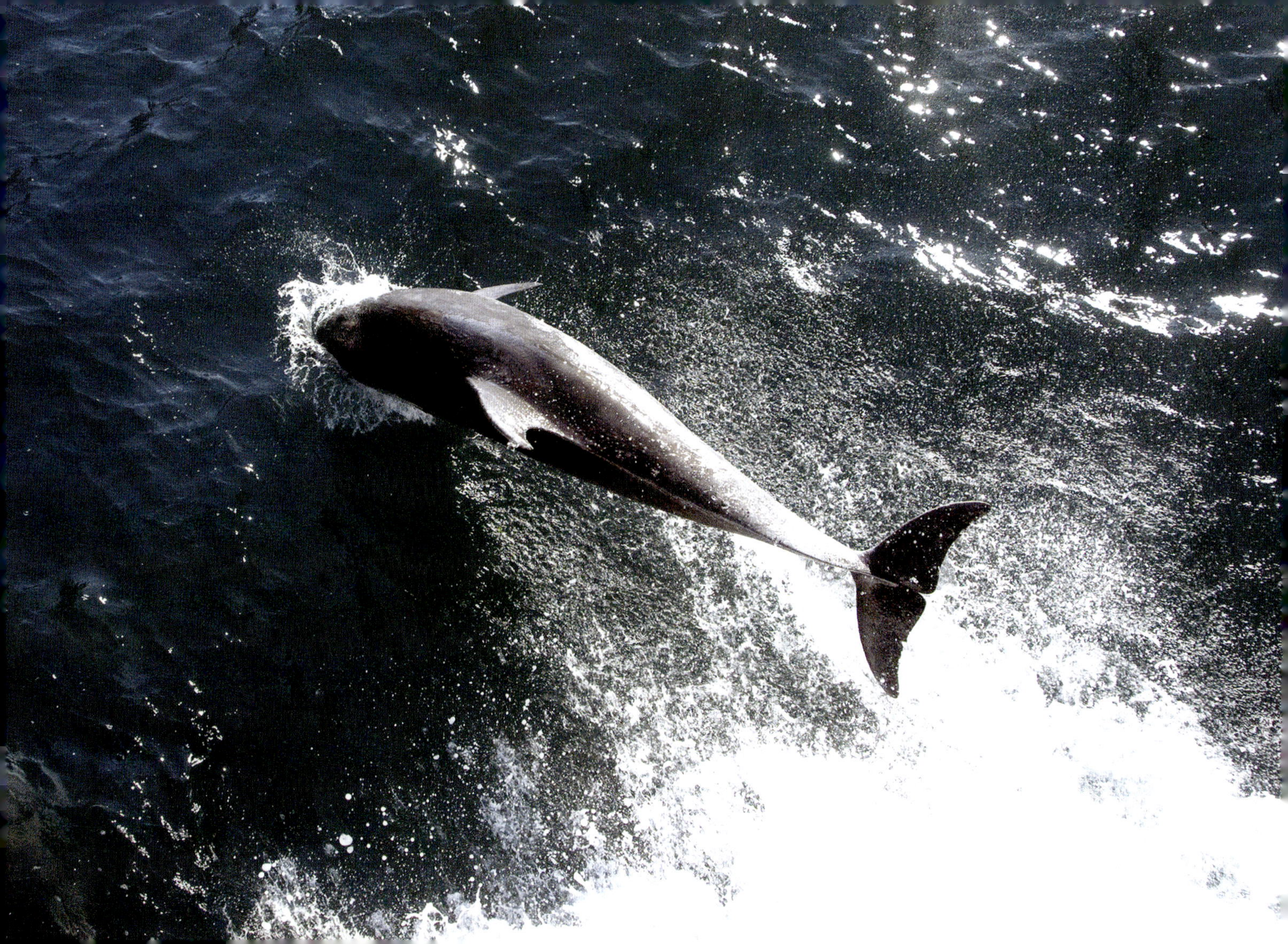

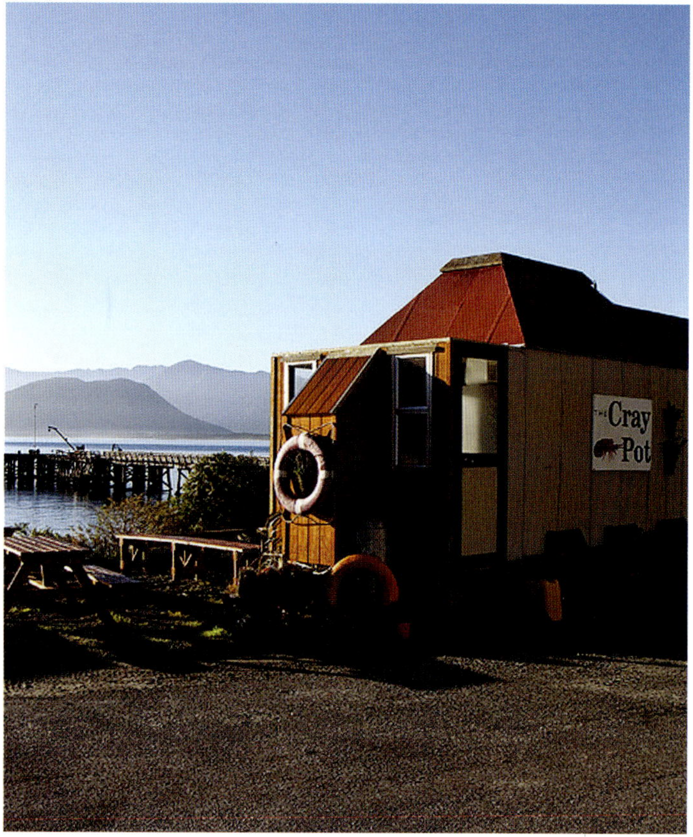

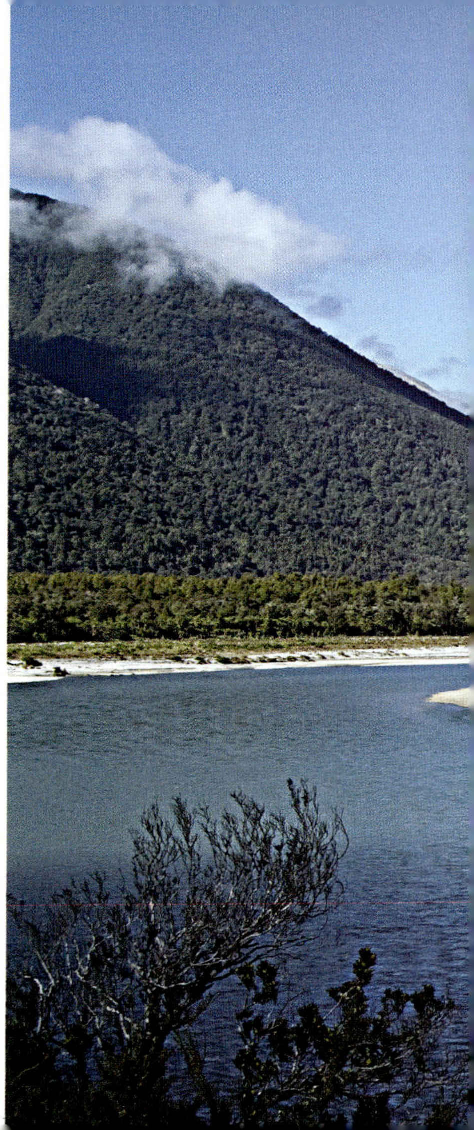

▲ It's a bit early for service here at the Cray Pot in Jackson Bay, but it's on our list for next time.

▶ The view from Arawhata Bridge, painted by nature – and my Nikon.

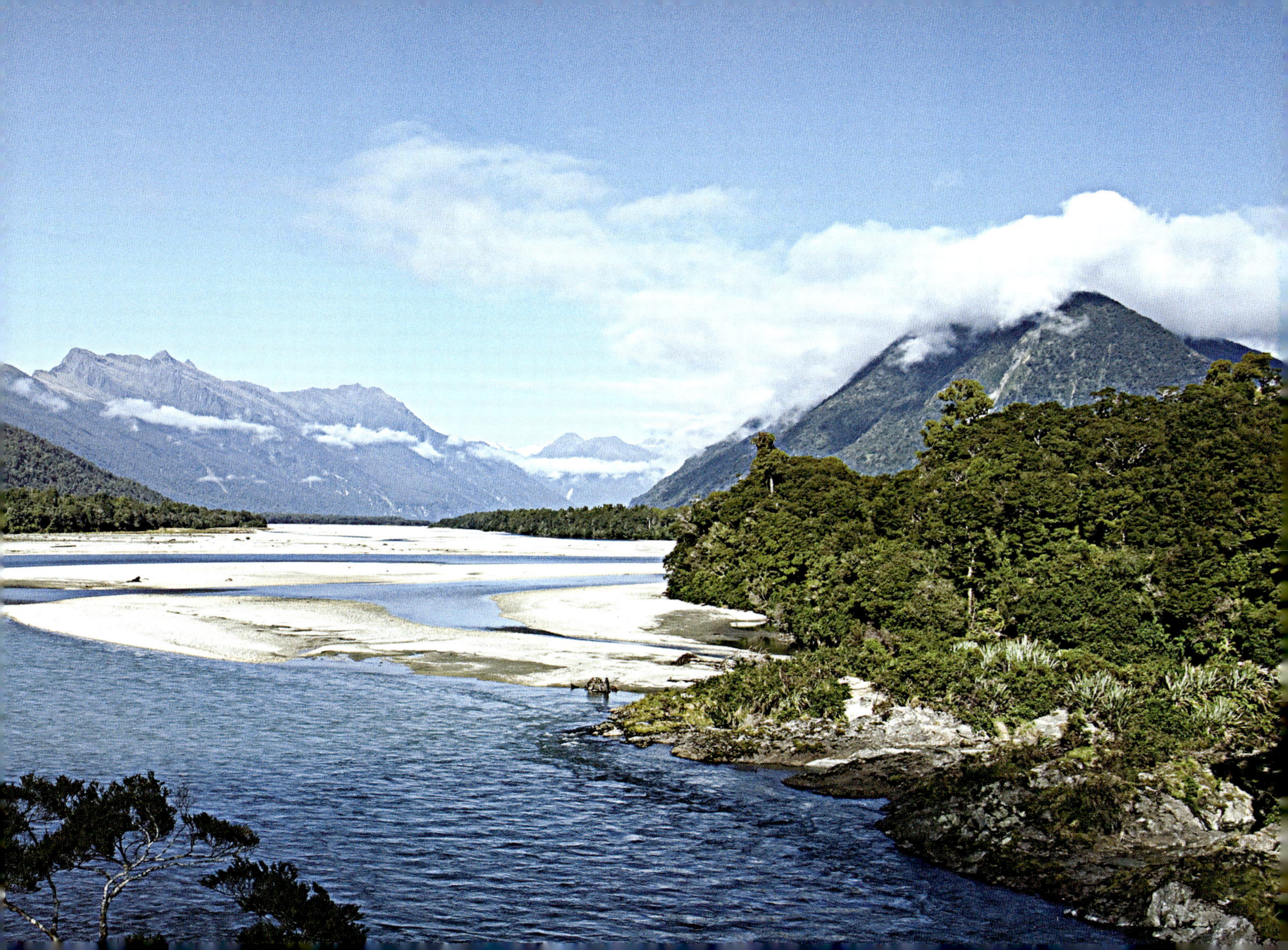

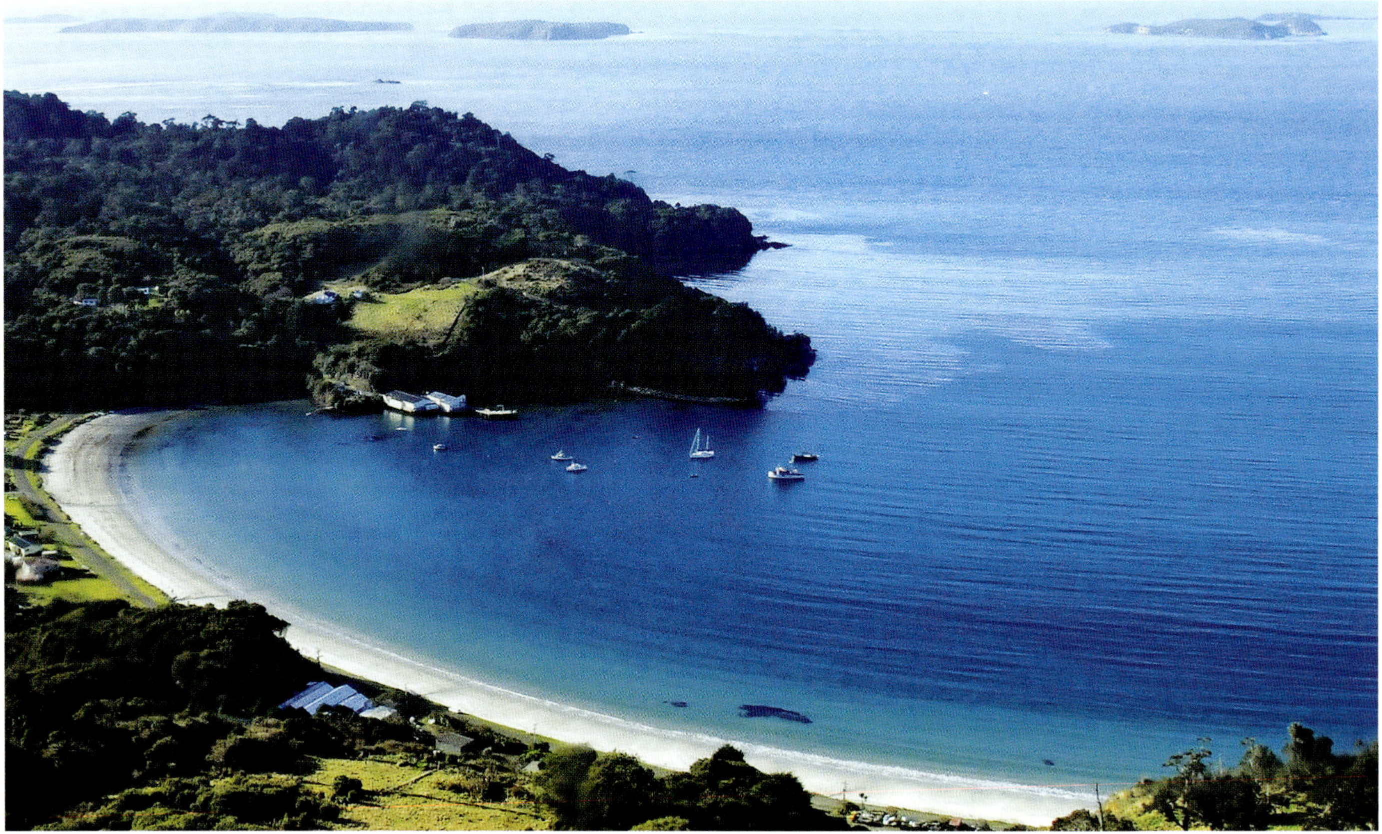

▲ Horseshoe Bay on Stewart Island has a surprisingly tropical look considering it's in the Far South.

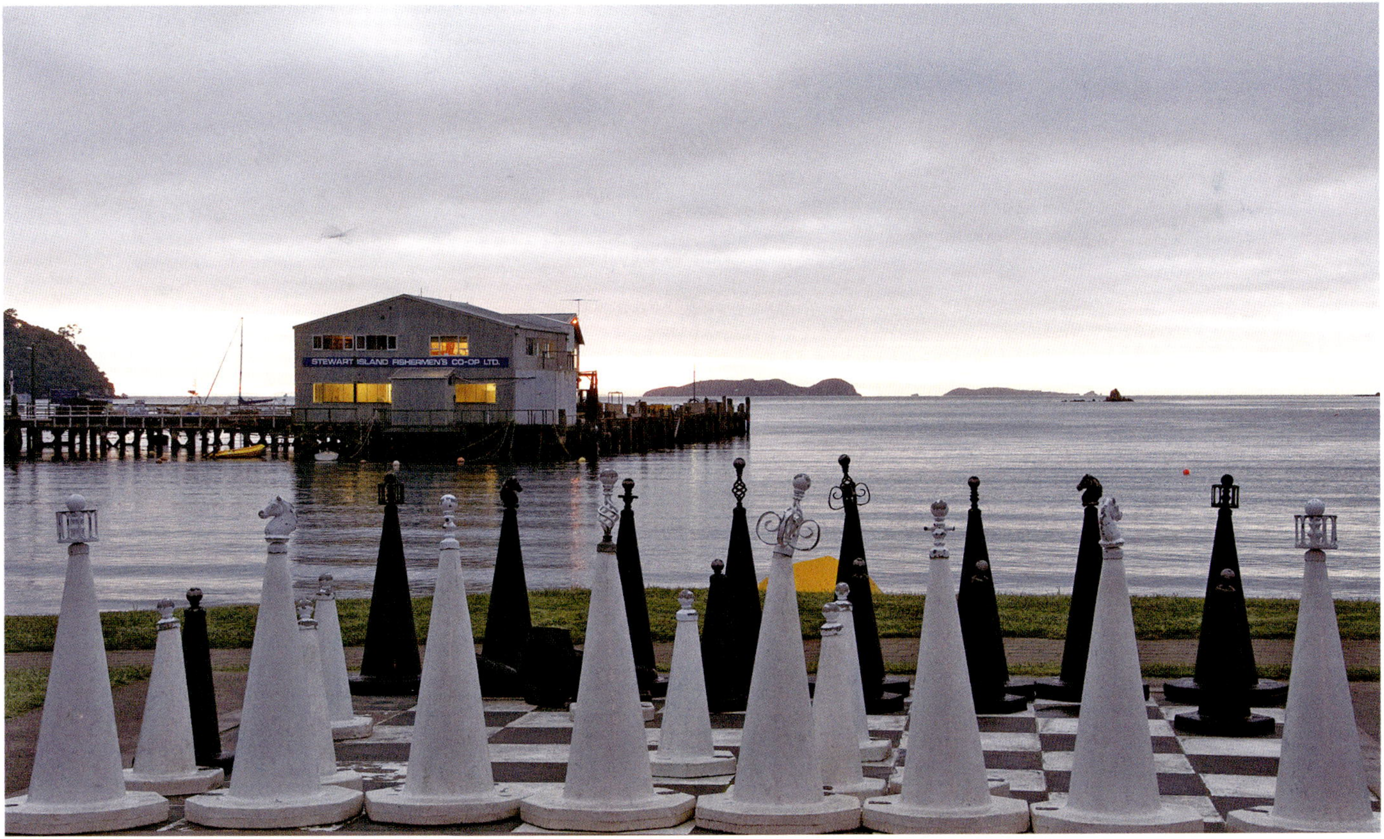

▲ Half Moon Bay, also on Stewart Island, is a southern paradise where the air is filled with the bird calls of kiwi, wood pigeons (kereru) and big green parakeets (kakariki).

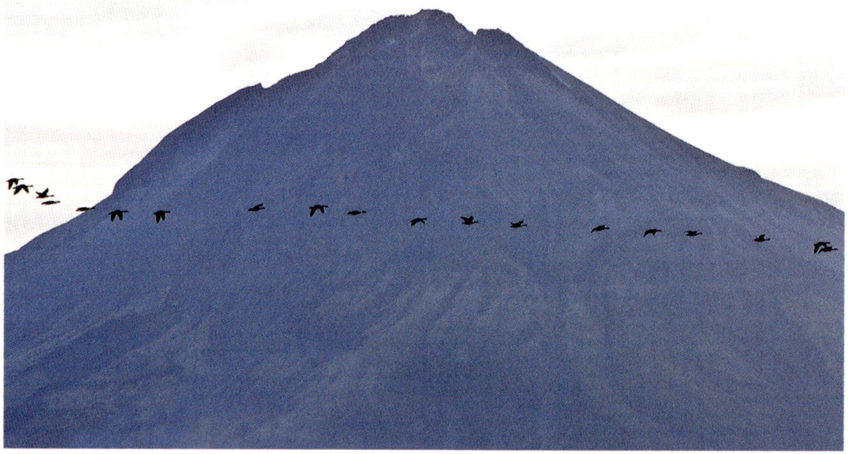

Migrating Canadian geese glide past Mount Taranaki (near where I call home).

First published in 2014 by New Holland Publishers (NZ) Ltd
Auckland • Sydney • London

www.newhollandpublishers.co.nz

218 Lake Road, Northcote, Auckland 0627, New Zealand
Unit 1, 66 Gibbes Street, Chatswood, NSW 2067, Australia
The Chandlery, Unit 114, 50 Westminster Bridge Road, London, SE1 7QY, United Kingdom

National Library of New Zealand Cataloguing-in-Publication Data

Looney, Fay.
The Real New Zealand / Fay Looney.
ISBN 978-1-86966-407-7
1. New Zealand—Pictorial works. I. Title.
919.300222—dc 23

10 9 8 7 6 5 4 3 2 1

Front cover: Lighthouse, Cape Reinga.
Back cover: Waka crews, Waitangi; letterbox, Awakino.

Publishing manager: Christine Thomson
Writer: Virgil Evetts
Editor: Renée Lang
Design: Fay Looney, Thomas Casey
Cover design: Thomas Casey

Colour reproduction by SC (Sang Choy) International Pte Ltd, Singapore.
Printed in China at Everbest Printing Co, on paper sourced from sustainable forests.